"*Blessings for Leaders* is a straight-forward account of how leaders can learn from the wisdom of Jesus. Dan provides insight into the daily challenges of leadership."

> —Cheryl Goodwin, CEO
> Family Resources, Inc., a regional not-for-profit
> serving the Quad Cities of Iowa and Illinois

"*Blessings for Leaders* is truly inspiring reading for those of us who are hungering for more profound leadership growth. Using the life and words of Jesus, Dan illustrates how we can pursue our missions in life while we effectively and authentically impact the world around us."

> —Marty Kurtz, CEO
> The Planning Center, Inc., Moline, Illinois and
> 2012 Chair, The Financial Planning Association

"*Blessings for Leaders* is an amazing book written for everyone who wishes to energize their faith and practice real leadership. Dan's book makes leadership very do-able!"

> —Clyde Mayfield
> Owner Greatest Grains on Earth
> Davenport, Iowa

Blessings for Leaders

Leadership Wisdom from the Beatitudes

Dan R. Ebener

LITURGICAL PRESS
Collegeville, Minnesota

www.litpress.org

Cover design by Stefan Killen Design.

A portion of chapter 6 is adapted from Dan R. Ebener, "On Becoming a Servant Leader: Seven Myths and Seven Paradoxes of Christian Leadership," *Sojourners* (February 2011): 33–34. Used with permission.

1   2   3   4   5   6   7   8

Library of Congress Control Number: 2012943792

ISBN 978-0-8146-3507-0 — ISBN 978-0-8146-3532-2 (e-book)

Matthew 5:1-12

When Jesus saw the crowds, he went up the mountain; and after he
sat down, his disciples came to him. Then he began to speak, and
taught them, saying:

Blessed are the poor in spirit,
   for theirs is the kingdom of heaven.
Blessed are those who mourn,
   for they will be comforted.
Blessed are the meek,
   for they will inherit the earth.
Blessed are those who hunger and thirst for righteousness,
   for they will be filled.
Blessed are the merciful,
   for they will receive mercy.
Blessed are the pure in heart,
   for they will see God.
Blessed are the peacemakers,
   for they will be called children of God.
Blessed are those who are persecuted for righteousness' sake,
   for theirs is the kingdom of heaven.

———

*To be a disciple of Jesus is to say yes to the Great Invitation to
come forth to follow and to learn the mission of Jesus (see Matt
4:18-22).*

*To be an apostle of Jesus is to say yes to the Great Commission
to go forth to lead and to teach the mission of Jesus (see Matt
28:16-20).*

Contents

Acknowledgments

To Amy Larson, my research assistant and colleague, for seeing this book as a mission.

To Mark Ridolfi, for teaching me the virtue of parsimony.

To Mary Frick, for sharing your grammatical wizardry.

To Joe Durepos, for coaching me through the first eight months of this book.

To Chuck Quilty, Laurie Hoefling, Suzanne Wiese, Clyde Mayfield, Micah Kiel, Eric Bauswell, Msgr. John Hyland, Barb Arland-Fye, Celine Klosterman, Glenn Leach, Frank Agnoli, Phil Hart, Laura Lortz, Debra Sullivan, Rebecca Peterson, Lonnie Mason, Angela Ode, and Tyla Cole, for providing critical and meaningful feedback on various drafts of this book.

To Trish Vanni, for leading me through the publishing stages of this book; and to Stephanie Lancour, Monica Schulzetenberg, and the good folks at Liturgical Press, for welcoming me as your colleague.

To Randy Richards, Megan Gisi, Ron Wastyn, Rick Dienesch, David O'Connell, Fred Smith, Linda Wastyn, George Hollins, Mary M. Schmidt, Monica Forret, Joe McCaffrey, and all my colleagues of Saint Ambrose University, for the ongoing dialogue about leadership.

To my students, who continuously challenge me to learn and grow.

To Jude West and Msgr. Marv Mottet, for mentoring me.

To Bishop Martin Amos, Msgr. John Hyland, Char Maaske, and all my colleagues at the Diocese of Davenport, for your ongoing support and opportunities to practice leadership.

To Sr. Laura Goedken, the diocesan Stewardship Commission, and all my stewardship friends.

To my colleagues and students at the Zagreb School of Economics and Management.

To my friends and colleagues around the world in peacemaking and social justice networks.

To my friends at Sojourners, for their permission to use the material in chapter 6.

To the vestry of Christ Episcopal Church, for inspiring this book at your leadership retreat.

To my racquetball buddies and walking partners, for giving me respite from this work.

And most of all: To De, Josh and Paula, Zach and Nikki, Luke, Jordan, and my whole family, for teaching me that life happens by being fully present to the moment.

—— Introduction ——

Blessings for Leaders

Imagine this scene: Jesus is teaching on a beautiful mountain-side. The area overlooks the scenic Sea of Galilee (see cover). He has just called the Twelve to *come, learn,* and *follow* as *disciples* (Matt 4:18-22). Now he is starting a three-year process of training his *followers* to become *leaders* who will *go, teach,* and *lead* (Matt 28:16-20) as *apostles.*

The script from the Gospel of Matthew gives us these five small bits of information just prior to Jesus' famous Sermon on the Mount (Matt 5:1-2):

- He draws away from the crowds. Jesus has been preaching, teaching in the synagogue, proclaiming the good news, healing the people of every disease and illness. Great crowds gather around him. His reputation is growing.

- He begins to walk up a mountain. He is near Capernaum, the town of Peter and Andrew, which is surrounded by the hills of Galilee. This is an opportunity for the disciples to spend quality time with their leader.

- He sits down. Sitting was a formal teaching position in that time and place. An important lesson is in the works.

- His disciples gather around him. Jesus is not teaching the masses. His core audience is his *disciples*, who will become his *apostles*.

- He begins to teach them, saying . . . What follows is the Sermon on the Mount, the most direct teachings of Jesus.

The young rabbi from Nazareth is about to change the course of human history. His message is a source of *uncommon wisdom* for the ages.

The next eight lines of the Gospel of Matthew (Matt 5:3-10) are known as the *Beatitudes*, the opening to the Sermon on the Mount, the heart of Jesus' teaching. They describe eight ways that God enters into our *human* lives and invites us into a *divine* relationship. They offer radical insight into Christian discipleship and the nature of leadership.

The Eight Beatitudes

1. *"Blessed are the poor in spirit."* The idea of poverty in spirit is counter-intuitive, which means counter to common thinking. The poor in spirit have an emptiness that can only be filled with God's presence. They yearn to be close to God. Leaders who are poor in spirit realize that they need God and others. God inspires the mission and vision for leadership. They understand that *without followers*, there are *no leaders*.

2. *"Blessed are those who mourn."* Leaders who mourn can learn to identify with the suffering of their people. Through *personal* mourning, they have the opportunity to cultivate empathy. They can develop character. They can grow in *wisdom* born of that experience. Through *collective* mourning, they can build a sense of community.

3. *"Blessed are the meek."* Leaders who are meek are paradoxically strong yet gentle, assertive yet cooperative, powerful yet

disciplined in the use of that power. The meek grasp the power of serving with both strength and gentleness. Power grows exponentially for leaders with the wisdom and the grace to accept blame and give away credit.

4. *"Blessed are those who hunger and thirst for righteousness."* Leaders who hunger for righteousness are right with God and just with the people. They grow in *credibility* because they can be believed. They build trust because they are *trustworthy*. They have integrity because they *integrate* what they practice with what they preach.

5. *"Blessed are the merciful."* Leading with mercy gives people the freedom to try new things and to take prudent risks. The merciful encourage people to remain open-minded. The merciful leader develops the full potential of the followers as future leaders. The merciful provide cover for their people to innovate and sometimes to fail.

6. *"Blessed are the pure in heart."* Leaders who strive for a pure heart are motivated *first to serve* and *then to lead*. They are servant leaders who share power with the people instead of grabbing power for themselves. They examine their life and leadership for a worthy mission to serve instead of leading with selfish desires and ulterior motives.

7. *"Blessed are the peacemakers."* Peacemakers seek peace, not artificial harmony. Peacemakers reconcile conflict by collaborating rather than avoiding, competing, or accommodating. They promote healthy conflict about ideas and solutions. They hold meetings to *problem solve* instead of meetings designed to inform or to persuade.

8. *"Blessed are those who are persecuted for righteousness."* Leaders who practice the virtues associated with the first seven Beatitudes will face criticism, opposition, and even persecution. Leading by the Beatitudes takes *courage*. It defies conventional wisdom. Leaders meet resistance to change with the clarity of a *shared vision*.

The eight Beatitudes suggest eight ways that God provides divine inspiration and invites us to become more fully human. It is interesting that God enters gently, patiently, and powerfully, but not with coercion. As St. Thomas Aquinas suggests, God influences with *love*, *truth*, and *beauty*.[1] What a great model for leadership! God invites, influences, and inspires us with unconditional love, everlasting truth, and overwhelming beauty:

1. Love: God loves us as a parent who will always be there.

2. Truth: God enlightens us with unconventional wisdom.

3. Beauty: God awes us with the splendors of creation.

The Ten Commandments, which receive much more attention than the Beatitudes, provide a *moral* foundation for society. The Ten Commandments suggest a starting point that is *necessary* but not *sufficient* for the people of God. The Beatitudes provide a *virtuous* foundation for discipleship. Their meaning is richer, the demands are deeper, and the motivation for those who live them is more intrinsic. The Greek word for *command* means to control a subject who is reluctant to comply or unwilling to follow. To command is to order a person without free will.

The Beatitudes are not commandments. Jesus is not commanding his disciples to live by them. He is teaching us the wisdom of living the blessed life of the Beatitudes.

Jesus *invites* us to discipleship through his Great Invitation to come and follow him. He *instructs* us with his Sermon on the Mount. He *inspires* us through his passion, death, and resurrection. And he *delegates* leadership responsibility to us through the Great Commission to go make disciples of all nations.

God has the power to command and coerce but chooses to influence instead. God influences through love, truth, and beauty. God is love. God is truth. God is beauty. Despite the almighty power, God offers us free will. God grants the *voluntary* choice to follow.

As leaders, we can choose to model God's influential ways. When in positions of authority, we can choose to coerce people or to influence them in loving, truthful, and beautiful ways. It may be tempting to control or coerce. *Coercion is not God's way. Nor is it leadership*. It may be management. It may be commandership. But it is not leadership.

Leadership and Management

Leadership is an interactive process where leaders and followers influence each other to bring about change. Leaders and followers move each other toward a *common goal*. According to author Joseph Rost, the word *influence* signifies a *voluntary* relationship between leaders and followers. Leadership is not coercive. It is *interactive*. The common goal is identified and articulated in the interactive process of influencing each other.

- *Leadership* is not positional. It can emerge from anywhere.

- *Management*, on the other hand, is an authority relationship that focuses on the day-to-day, administrative work of an organization, an important function but not identical to leadership. By definition, management is positional.

- Those in positions of authority are not always leaders. Some are *bosses*. Many are *managers*. When we rely solely on positional authority, we are *not* leading.

- Those in positions of leadership *can* be leaders. When we rely on influence, we lead. Bosses do not have to be bossy. They can become leaders when they choose to influence and persuade instead of coerce and control.

- Leadership is a role or a function, not a person or a position.

Managers put structure into our lives. Leaders breathe new life into our structures. Both leadership and management functions are necessary for effective organizations.

The *essence of leadership* is this: Leaders bring about change. They feel passionate about something that needs to change. They influence others to join them in creating and carrying out a strategy to change it. They realize they cannot do it by themselves. Then they develop their followers into leaders because the really big things need many leaders.

Blessings for Leaders

The Beatitudes are *blessings for leaders* because they provide wisdom for leadership. The word *beatitude* is Latin for *blessing*.

> *The Beatitudes are eight bold statements about life that offer astonishing insight into leadership.*

The wisdom of the Beatitudes can be gleaned from a close reading and rich understanding of the psalms, proverbs, and prophets.

The blessings of the Beatitudes are paradoxical, which means they appear to hold a contradiction but have a deeper sense of truth to them. The blessings of the Beatitudes are granted now and in the future. The kingdom of God is declared in the Beatitudes as *already but not yet*. The Beatitudes include a means and an end. The blessings are *pathways* (the means) and *promises* for the future (the end).

The first paradox of each Beatitude lies in the *pathway* to the blessing. According to the Beatitudes, to become spiritually poor, compassionate, meek, just, merciful, pure of heart, peaceful, and persecuted is to be *blessed*. At first impression, this might look like a list of character flaws for leaders. Anything *poor* is usually considered the bane of human existence. In these Beatitudes, Jesus is challenging our assumptions, breaking down our stereotypes, and suggesting new ideas that are counter-intuitive and new behaviors that are counter-cultural.

The second paradox lies in the *promise* of the blessing. The blessings of the Beatitudes are counter-cultural because they run counter to the cultural norms that value fame and fortune. The blessings of the Beatitudes include consolation, justice, mercy, and peace, all signs of the kingdom of God. This topples the scales of our cultural values. Our society preaches *external* rewards for human excellence, not *eternal* ones. Living and leading by the Beatitudes fits the norms of a higher kingdom. Conventional wisdom would suggest that personal honor, glory, recognition, control, and authority might be results sought by a successful leader.

The third paradox to the Beatitudes is that being poor of spirit, compassionate, meek, just, merciful, pure of heart, peaceful, and persecuted can bring true joy in the here and now *and* divine blessings in the future. The Beatitudes promise a place of fulfillment where the kingdom of God is ours both here and now *and* it will be ours in eternity. To think either/or when the answer is both/and is what we call a *false dichotomy*. The blessings of justice, mercy, peace, and other signs of the kingdom will be "on earth as it is in heaven" (Matt 6:10), to quote the prayer that Jesus taught, the Our Father.

Purpose of This Book

The Beatitudes of Matthew's gospel offer spiritual and practical insight to develop the *character* needed for both leaders and followers. They are offered by Jesus to his disciples—his followers, whom he is training to be leaders—at the very start of his Sermon on the Mount.

The purpose of this book is to consider the wisdom Jesus provides in the Beatitudes so that we might lead people to holier lives. The world desperately needs leadership! The Beatitudes are not a textbook for leadership. That would be an overstatement. They provide valuable insights that we can use to examine our lives, monitor our behaviors, and build the inner qualities we need to become human beings capable of leadership.

The Gospel of Matthew is a leadership gospel. It will be used consistently throughout this book. It is ideal for this book because leadership is a major theme for Matthew. Jesus is developing followers into leaders, students into teachers, and disciples into apostles:

Discipleship and apostleship are the two bookends of Matthew's gospel. Early in his gospel, we are called to followership in the Great Invitation to come, see, learn, and follow—to become *disciples*

Disciples follow, learn, and then become apostles. Apostles lead, teach, and make more disciples.

of Jesus (Matt 4:18-22). In the final paragraph, we are commissioned to leadership in the Great Commission to go, tell, teach, and lead—to become *apostles* who make disciples of all nations (Matt 28:16-20). Between these bookends, we are treated to inspirational stories of healing, challenging, interacting, teaching, and the saving actions of the passion, death, and resurrection of Jesus.

Each chapter of this book will be shaped around the meaning of one Beatitude. We will look at Holy Scripture and see what Jesus teaches us about the *internal* journey required of leadership. And then we will look at the *external* challenges of leadership, applying the wisdom of that Beatitude to the skills and behaviors demanded of leadership.

We will explore the message of Jesus for the *wisdom of the ages*. We will gain insight into how we nurture the values, practice the virtues, and develop the *inner* character to change the way we live, lead, manage, and follow. Then we will consider the *modern-day lessons* we have learned about the *outer* challenges of leadership, such as mission, vision, core values, emotional intelligence, conflict resolution, trust-building, and teamwork.

This book will explain some of the skills needed for leadership. As author Robert Katz points out, leaders rely more on *people* skills, such as listening, dialogue, and facilitation, and *conceptual* skills, such as visioning, strategic planning, and adaptive thinking. Many are promoted into positions of authority because of *technical* expertise, not because of people or conceptual skills.

This book focuses on how Jesus developed the *inner character* of his disciples to prepare them for the *outer challenges* of apostleship. I will approach the words and stories of Jesus as a sociologist. I teach leadership, which is rooted in the social sciences and philosophy. I will explore the Beatitudes for the virtues associated with each one. Then I will discuss these virtues as they relate to various leadership styles, theories, and concepts.

We will ask ourselves the following question: How can we walk in the footsteps of Jesus as we face the leadership challenges of our workplaces, communities, and families?

The *leadership skills* aspect of the book is augmented by a website where additional materials will be updated regularly: www.blessingsforleaders.com.

www.blessingsforleaders.com

Endnote
1. *Summa Theologica* I, q. 5, a. 4, ad. 1; q. 16, a. 5; and q. 20.

Chapter 1

Wisdom

Blessed are the poor in spirit, for theirs is the kingdom of heaven.
—*Matthew 5:3*

The wisdom of the Beatitudes begins with this simple message: Place your trust in God. Surrender your will humbly to God. Be strong in your faith. Jesus calls this *poverty of spirit.*

The first Beatitude builds upon the first commandment: "I am the LORD your God . . . you shall have no other gods before me" (Exod 20:2-3). The essence of this Beatitude is a close relationship with God. The poor in spirit recognize they are poor without God. They discern the will of God instead of forcing their own will. They accept that they are not always in control.

We are what we seek. The poor in spirit are on an intense search for spirituality. They are looking for authentic ways to be of service to God and others. Poverty creates a vacuum that desperately needs to be filled. Poverty of spirit creates a spiritual vacuum that can only be filled by a close proximity to God. Like water flowing down a mountain, seeking the lowest point, poverty of spirit seeks God's presence, grace, and blessings. The poor in spirit are prayerfully discerning the will of God for a *mission* to do God's work.

The poor in spirit empty themselves from the *inner* desires for the *exterior* rewards of life. They find the wisdom in God's presence and recognize the providence of God's hand in the events around them. They pray. They open themselves up to the power of the Holy Spirit.

The poor in spirit welcome the providence of God in their lives.

The rich in spirit are full of themselves. They seek fame, fortune, and material comforts. Wealth of spirit is like a cup turned upside down. Water poured into that cup just bounces away. As we turn our cup right side up, the grace, gifts, and wisdom of God can flow into our lives. This is our conversion point. To become poor in spirit by putting God and others first is the first step on our faithful journey to live and lead by the Beatitudes.

How Did Jesus Teach This?

"This is the one to whom I will look, to the humble and contrite in spirit" (Isa 66:2).

Jesus suggests that poverty of spirit holds the *key to his kingdom.* The second half of this Beatitude states, "for theirs is the kingdom of heaven" (Matt 5:3). The poor in spirit are seeking justice, mercy, and peace so that God's kingdom can be built *on earth as in heaven.*

Poor in spirit describes the crowds that followed Jesus. Many were sick, blind, or lame. They needed God. When Jesus began the Beatitudes with "Blessed are the poor in spirit," he was describing many of the people who followed him at that time. They had spiritual as well as material needs. They fulfilled both needs in Jesus. Their healing was assured because, as Jesus put it, "Your faith has made you well" (Matt 9:22). They had full confidence in God.

The poor, the sick, the blind, and the lame experience a more intense need for God. They welcome God's spirit into their lives. They embrace God's presence. They love God with their whole heart. They have fewer distractions and diversions. They live the spiritual life.

The rich in spirit in the time of Jesus were the religious leaders who condemned Jesus: the scribes and Pharisees (Matt 23). They lived beyond reproach. They were the epitome of hypocrisy and self-righteousness. They endorsed *the letter* but not *the spirit* of the law. They capitalized on every opportunity to contradict the message of Jesus or to trick him into a mistake.

Jesus cured the sick on the Sabbath (Matt 12:9-12). The scribes and Pharisees criticized Jesus for this. They complained that Jesus and his disciples were picking grains of wheat to eat on the Sabbath. Jesus explained that even on the Sabbath, people had to eat. The sick had to be cured. The human needs of the people are more important than the letter of the law.

Poverty of Spirit in Times of Crisis

Interestingly, it is through times of crisis that we are offered the opportunity to grow spiritually and become poorer in spirit.

9/11

Consider the mood following the tragic events of September 11, 2001. People mourned and prayed together. Leaders spoke with great conviction. The people felt a sense of mission. Churches filled up. The world responded with compassion. We understood our own human weakness, our frailty as a human family and our incapacity to solve problems of this magnitude by ourselves. We turned to God and to each other. *We grew in poverty of spirit.*

> *Poverty of spirit grows in times of crisis, such as war, natural disaster, human tragedy, economic stress, or political transition.*

Most Americans can remember where they were on the morning of 9/11. I was teaching a Masters of Organizational Leadership (MOL) strategic planning class at the Rock Island (IL) Arsenal, a military base. A friend of mine, Fred Smith, was visiting as a guest speaker. He is a strategic planner. I asked Fred for an update on what was happening in New York. He told us that both twin towers had been hit. We were all shocked that what had seemed like a terrible accident earlier that morning was turning into something much more tragic. *On September 11, we were poorer in spirit.*

In times of crisis, my first instinct is usually to move right into action. I am inclined to *do* something. But occasionally, God empties me of such foolishness and fills me with poverty in spirit. I remember to pray. On 9/11, I asked my MOL class if I could lead them in prayer, and everyone agreed. The words of prayer reminded us that regardless of how strong we think we are, we need the presence, providence, and movement of God in our lives.

The Soviet Union

I had the opportunity to visit the former Soviet Union in 1990, a time when policy reforms like *perestroika* (restructuring) and *glasnost* (openness) were being introduced by President Mikhail Gorbachev. I was in the USSR as part of a US delegation to assist the Russian Orthodox churches in setting up social services for the poor and needy. The religious community had been unable to organize services for the people under Communist rule.

It was a time of crisis, change, and confusion. Imagine a society trying to make a transition from driving on the right side of the road to the left side of the road. Now imagine making that transition *gradually*! That was the chaos we felt during our 1990 visit.

It was also a time of exuberance. Churches were reopening after being shut down for decades. It was a time of *opportunity*. Our delegation visited churches brimming with people at all hours of the day and week. I met people eager to practice their faith and bursting with confidence. They had a newfound sense of purpose. *They were poor in spirit.*

Nicaragua

One of my most profound experiences with poverty in spirit was my 1986 visit to Nicaragua. I led a mission group of ten people with Witness for Peace. The war between the Sandinistas and the US-backed *contras*, or counter-revolutionaries, was in full force. Our goal was to stop the war, one village at a time. Our mission was to create a peaceful presence and to live in *solidarity* with the people who were caught in the middle of that war.

My group was in the small village of Jalapa, near the Honduras border. We heard gunfire in the surrounding mountains every day. I slept on a dirt floor for two weeks, staying with a young family whose teenage

The poor in spirit feel indebted, not entitled.

sons were fighting in the war. With this family, I studied the Bible. I prayed with them every day. Surrounded by war and poverty, the words of Scripture became more real to me than ever before. They took on new and deeper meaning.

One day, three teenage soldiers from Jalapa were killed. A group of young and heavily armed soldiers brought the three bodies into town. There was no priest. Several of the men in the village acted as deacons and catechists, including the father of the family with whom I was staying. They asked me to lead the community in prayer at the wake and funeral.

Hundreds of villagers gathered for the wake service. The people mourned and prayed. They brought flowers. As our small group approached, the crowd parted and we passed through. We entered the living room of a small adobe house that served as the home of one of the victims. The families welcomed us. The three bodies were displayed in simple wooden boxes. I led the people in prayer. As I prayed, I felt an intensity in God's presence. God was right there! I prayed more passionately than I had ever prayed before. *At that moment, we were poor in spirit.*

The next day, the entire village turned out for the funeral. The adobe church was overflowing. People spilled over the rickety wooden balcony. Children sat in open windows. We prayed for the dead and for an end to the war, violence, and poverty. After the funeral, the pallbearers lifted the three wooden caskets on their shoulders, and we walked in funeral procession to the cemetery. We prayed and sang church hymns all the way.

The sights, sounds, and smells of that day are vivid memories: The sight of mothers mourning for their children. Children mourning for their siblings. And villagers mourning for their friends. The sound of people lifting up prayers and singing hymns. The smell of the earth when we arrived at the three freshly dug holes at the cemetery. *We were poor in spirit.* We were in need of God. We could feel God's presence.

What Is the Leadership Message?

Leadership Matters

The wisdom of the Beatitudes was shared by Jesus with his disciples, his leaders-in-training. He was teaching the *discipline* it takes to move from *followers* to *leaders*, from *students* to *teachers*, from *disciples* to *apostles*. This first Beatitude was the first lesson in this training, the opening line to his Sermon on the Mount.

Jesus intended these counter-intuitive lessons for all who respond to his Great Invitation to *come, learn,* and *follow*, and his Great Commission to *go, teach,* and *lead*.

The Beatitudes describe eight qualities that make us worthy of the kingdom of God: the pathways and the promises of each blessing. The poor in spirit open themselves up to the *wisdom* that can be discerned from the virtuous life Jesus taught in the Beatitudes.

Leadership begins with poverty of spirit. Leadership is an interactive process where leaders and followers influence each other to reach a *common goal*. Leaders have to realize that *without other people*, it is not leadership. *Without free will*, it is not leadership. God grants us free will and then invites, inspires, and influences us to surrender our free will to God's will.

Blessed are Leaders who are Poor in Spirit

This is our *model for leadership*—to intrinsically motivate others to follow us. When we rely on command, control, and coercion, we are more likely to instill fear than love among those being led. It is more difficult to build trust and to encourage kindness in a culture of fear.

The road to spiritual poverty is an inward journey. The Beatitudes provide a reflection guide to cultivate the inner qualities, moral fiber, and personal disposition we need for leadership. The Beatitudes provide wisdom that can guide us as we examine ourselves for leadership.

The poor in spirit build inner strength. As we become spiritually poor, we develop strength of character. Strength of conviction. Strength of community with others. Strength of commitment to a mission. Strength of a close relationship with God. This internal strength enables us to face the external challenges of leadership.

The *inward journey* of leadership focuses on the *how and why* in order to become human beings who are worthy to lead. The *outward journey* focuses on *what we do* as leaders. Our first lesson on the outward challenges flows out of poverty of spirit: the *mission* of leadership.

Missionary Zeal

According to Matthew, the mission of Jesus is the fulfillment of these words from Isaiah: "Here is my servant, whom I have chosen, my beloved, with whom my soul is well pleased. I will put my Spirit upon him, and he will proclaim justice to the Gentiles" (Matt 12:18; cf. Isa 42:1-2).

The *Year of Jubilee* is what Jesus was proclaiming. The Year of Jubilee is the restoration of justice. According to Isaiah, it would be advanced in the coming of the Messiah: "The spirit of the Lord GOD is upon me, because the LORD has anointed me; he has sent me to bring good news to the oppressed, to bind up the brokenhearted, to proclaim liberty to the captives, and release to the prisoners; to proclaim the year of the LORD's favor [Year of Jubilee]" (Isa 61:1-2).

> *Jesus proclaims the Year of Jubilee as his mission (Matt 12:18). This is the good news.*

We need to find our mission. When we establish a mission as the source of our power, strength, and energy, we become poorer in spirit. We are not driven by the need for *personal* power, prestige, and privilege. We *socialize* the power by spreading it around. This

The poor in spirit focus on a mission. frees us up to be totally devoted to a mission greater than ourselves instead of pushing our own agenda.

Mission goes beyond the bottom line. Leaders who can articulate the social purpose behind their enterprise can add meaning to the work and actually enhance the financial bottom line. Creating a sense of mission transforms the way we look at our organizations: Pharmaceutical companies are *finding cures for diseases*. Agricultural businesses are *feeding the world*. Engineers are *creating solutions to our energy dependence*. Highway construction companies are *improving public safety*. By reframing our work as something that contributes to the common good, we add purpose to our lives and to those who work with us.

Mission Statements

A mission statement helps us see the bigger picture and understand how our day-to-day work is contributing to a higher cause, something that benefits society.

For more on mission, visit:

WWW

www.blessingsforleaders.com

When writing a mission statement, *make the process very interactive*. Set up group forums so that all stakeholders have an opportunity to participate. Explain the three components of a mission statement (*business, purpose, and values*) and give examples.

The interactive process of writing a mission statement can be more beneficial than the final product (the mission statement itself). Seeing and hearing your colleagues talk about respect, wellness, safety, service, beauty, collaboration, or innovation can be a very powerful experience. Listening to each other as we explain how our work contributes to the common good is very inspiring. When done in a participative manner, the process of writing a mission statement builds camaraderie, cohesion, and commitment to the mission itself.

Conclusion

Poverty of spirit reminds us of the need for God and others in order to accomplish our mission. Jesus modeled poverty of spirit by spending forty days in the desert before he began his public ministry (Matt 4:1-11). He described poverty of spirit in the prayer he taught us, the Our Father (Matt 6:9-13). He established righteousness with God and others as his core mission.

Mission is the soul of the organization. It lives on. It survives the current members of an organization. It can be woven into the fabric of an organization as the heart of the culture. Leaders inspire their people by exuding *missionary zeal* for the purpose of their organization.

People hunger for a sense of purpose. They want to have an impact. Some of us work day in and day out without reflecting on what contribution we are making to the common

> *The heart of a mission statement is purpose.*

good of society. Purpose reinforces the *dignity* of workers and the *dignity* of our work. It builds determination and gives meaning to the forty-plus hours that we spend each week at work.

Mission is a source of wisdom for the leader and for the people. A sense of mission inspires people to go *above and beyond* the call of duty. A statement of mission articulates the need to go *below and beyond* the financial bottom line. It creates a new bottom line.

Missionary zeal is one example of the leadership wisdom that we can glean from the Beatitudes. Wisdom is more than information. *Wisdom is insight born of experience.* Wisdom grows when we place our trust in God, recognize that we do not have all the answers, collaborate with others for solutions, and reflect on our experiences in life and leadership.

Discussion Questions (*"Blessed are the poor in spirit"*)

1. Think about times when you felt the need for God the most in your life. Were those times of loss or crisis? What can you learn from those times?

2. What is your mission in life? Is it apparent to the people you touch?

3. As a leader, how well do you use mission to keep your followers intrinsically motivated?

—— *Chapter 2* ——

Empathy

Blessed are those who mourn, for they will be comforted.
—*Matthew 5:4*

The first Beatitude *fuels the spirit*. This second Beatitude *cultivates the heart*. The human heart brings oxygen to the arteries and produces energy. The leader's heart generates empathy for the people and passion for the mission. Leaders must provide bursts of energy.

We can grow in strength from the experience of mourning. Mourning exercises the muscles of the heart. We develop resilience. We remember what is most important in life. We empathize with the pain of others. We develop a more durable capacity to mourn again.

Mourning also enhances our poverty of spirit because it enables us to realize our self-limitations. We are exposed to our vulnerability. We are confronted with the reality that we are finite human beings. It is in times of greatest mourning that we are most likely to acknowledge our dependence on God. Our wholehearted search for God becomes even more intense.

> *To mourn is to reach out to the divine and to become fully human.*

Mourning and poverty in spirit have a reciprocal effect on each other. They reinforce each other. The people of Jalapa, Nicaragua, mourned the loss of their sons and in the process they became poorer in spirit. Mourners *become* poor in spirit. They can grow in empathy.

Mourning can warm the heart of even the coldhearted. Some are unable, unwilling, or reluctant to mourn precisely because their hearts are cold and their spirits are frozen. They are numb to the suffering of others. They think only of themselves. It takes a close personal loss for the coldhearted to mourn. Those occasions are rare. They have few close relationships.

How Did Jesus Teach This?

At the sight of the crowds, his heart was moved with compassion (see Matt 9:36).

The incarnation—a divine person becoming fully human—is a clear demonstration of the empathy of Jesus. By fully entering the human condition, Jesus was able to relate to our pain and become the Suffering Servant that was foretold by the prophet Isaiah (Isa 52:13–53:12).

Jesus cured the sick (Matt 4:23). The people who followed Jesus were *those who mourn.* They were poor in many ways. They experienced injustice. Jesus listened and responded with empathy. Healing was at the center of Jesus' ministry. He brought comfort to those who mourn.

Jesus fed the five thousand (Matt 14:13-21). Just prior to this famous story, Jesus learned of the death of his first cousin, John the Baptist. He withdrew from the crowds and looked for a solitary place for some quiet, reflective time. Yet the people followed, bringing their sick to him. Moved by compassion, Jesus healed. Because this was such a remote place, the people grew hungry without food. So Jesus fed the five thousand with a few loaves and fishes.

Tired and weary, poor in spirit, mourning the loss of his cousin, looking for solitude, Jesus showed compassion. He listened and responded to the needs of the people. Jesus showed from personal experience that he could understand and relate to the suffering of the people. His empathy moved him into action. He healed the sick and fed the hungry.

Collective Mourning

The Lord hears the cry of the poor, hungry, and righteous (see Ps 34).

Mourning enhances our relationships. Times of mourning bring people together. Our friends, colleagues, and loved ones suffer with us. When we mourn together as a family or community, we can grow in empathy and love for each other. These relationships strengthen our endurance during times of mourning. We can grow in wisdom born of suffering.

Several of my closest friends have died very young. Mourning for them enhanced my relationships with others. Their wakes and funerals became a time for collective mourning when whole communities gathered and new relationships were formed.

J.C.

When my friend Jeff Cottingham was diagnosed with terminal cancer in 1990, he became *poorer in spirit.* He had always been very close to God and was passionate about practicing his faith. Because he shared initials with Jesus Christ, we called him J.C. In fact, when everyone else was asking, "What would Jesus do?" we modified the question to "What would J.C. do?" because so often, it was the same answer.

His cancer seemed to strengthen his faith life as he realized his great need for God. He turned his two years of cancer treatment into the holiest time of his life. While everyone else was in mourning for J.C., he remained focused on God and others. Dozens of people visited his hospital room and he ministered to them. They wanted to talk about how he was doing, but J.C. invariably turned the conversation to focus on others. From his deathbed, he was preaching the Gospel, praying for others, and modeling great faith to all of us.

As my friend Mark Ridolfi put it, "When I visited J.C., I never knew what I was going to say, how I would react, how in the world I could possibly be helpful. But every time, J.C. bridged the gap so eloquently, so spiritually, so simply. I learned from a dying man how to be compassionate and engaged. I left rewarded, not drained."

J.C.'s death in 1993 was particularly tough because his two children were very young: Bethany was four years old and Christian was almost two. It was important for them to get to know their father through his friends. Along with other friends, my wife De and I stepped up. We treat Bethany and Christian like a niece and nephew. J.C.'s wife Rhea became an even closer friend. We celebrated Christmas and birthdays together. We went camping every summer with a large group of J.C.'s friends. The kids would hear stories of their father around the campfire. We went to ballgames together. We became family to each other.

My relationships with Bethany and Christian deepened after their father's death. My wife and I continue to be active in their lives. Our sons Josh and Zach call and visit Beth and Chris as young adults. Our relationships continue to grow out of mourning for the death of J.C.

Martha

Wakes and funerals seem particularly tough when the person who died is at the peak of life or in the early stages of life. There is a lot of wisdom to the saying that children are supposed to bury their parents, not the other way around. My parents—Bob and Anne Ebener—were blessed with five boys and six girls. My sister Martha died as an infant when I was twelve years old. My folks pulled us out of school that day. We gathered together at home, knelt around my parents' bedroom, and prayed the rosary. Prayer comforted us during our time of mourning.

We can also mourn *vicariously* through others. At my sister Martha's wake, we stood by her casket as we greeted friends and neighbors. That was painful. The hardest part was seeing the emotional impact on my mother. She burst into tears when we all had to say our final goodbyes to Martha. The memory of that moment is still painful. However, praying and standing together in that funeral parlor pulled us together as a family.

Ben

In 2007, my nephew Ben Ebener was killed in a car accident. It was a tragic loss. Ben was only twenty-five years old, a beloved member of our family. All nine of my brothers and sisters, my folks, and most of Ben's twenty-three first cousins turned out for the wake and funeral.

Relationships Matter

Once again, I experienced the pain we live vicariously through others. The death of my nephew Ben was a tough loss for me personally. But it was even tougher seeing my brother Jim grieve the loss of his son, and my godchild Emily lose her brother, and my wife De lose her godson, and my sons Josh and Zach grieve the loss of their cousin. Each of these relationships added another layer to my grief.

Our family bonds were deepened through our collective mourning. In many ways, Ben's death brought our family closer together. Those bonds strengthen us for the dark moments when death, illness, or loss disrupts our lives and breaks open the myth of our invulnerability.

God Works Miracles through Our Relationships

The healing ministry of Jesus continues today. It is one of life's great mysteries. We experience an illness. We become poorer in spirit. We grow in empathy. We deepen our relationships. We pray. And sometimes our prayers are answered with miraculous cures.

Spinal Meningitis

When I was seven months old, I experienced a near-fatal bout with spinal meningitis. The doctors gave up all hope for my survival. They quarantined me in a small hospital room where my mother stayed with me twenty-four hours a day for seventeen days.

I recently asked my mother what she did all that time she spent with me as a baby in an isolated hospital room, with no television, radio, or cell phone. Not surprisingly, *she prayed.* Knowing my mother, I also had to ask, "Which prayers?" And she told me she prayed to the Infant Jesus of Prague. This puzzled me. I asked her why, and she said simply because I was an infant and the Infant of Prague has been credited with many miraculous cures.

Empathy leads to understanding, which leads to action.

The medical miracle of my survival from spinal meningitis was actually more *relational* and less magical than it may sound. My mother's prayers had a profound impact on Dr. George Lucas, our family doctor, who happened to be a friend of my folks.

As my father tells the story, Dr. Lucas grew very concerned that my mother was going to be devastated when I died. He was *mourning* for my mother. In his mind, my death was inevitable. In my mother's mind, that was *not* going to happen! My mother's prayers gave her hope. Her hope and persistence inspired Dr. Lucas to take a medical risk and try something new. He said to my father, "You know, Bob, there is this new medicine on the market called penicillin . . . " We know now this is the correct treatment for spinal meningitis.

The difference between hope and optimism is important here. *Optimism* is looking at the data and expecting a positive outcome. *Hope* expects a positive outcome *despite* the facts. No amount of expert information from the doctors could extinguish my mother's hope. My mother's prayers gave her hope. Her hope inspired Dr. Lucas into action.

God works through people. And people work through relationships in the performance of some miracles. My parents were close friends with Dr. Lucas. He had delivered all eleven of my mother's children. He was competent. But it was his *relationship* with my parents that moved him with *compassion* so he could play his part in the miracle that saved my life.

In the summer of 2011, I traveled to the Czech Republic to visit the shrine to the Infant of Prague to give thanks for this miracle. It was an incredible day of prayer, reflection, and visiting with the monks who minister to the pilgrims who come there. It gave me an opportunity to prayerfully thank God, and to thank my mother for her faith, her prayers, and her leadership.

Blessed are
Leaders who
Mourn

N
W   E
S

What Is the Leadership Message?

Dr. Lucas showed empathetic leadership. Because of his relationship with my parents, Dr. Lucas was moved by my illness. He was inspired by my mother's leadership. His mourning turned to *empathy*. His empathy spurred him to *action*. His actions saved my life.

Mourning forms our hearts and shapes our character for leadership. Experiences of mourning are opportunities to build empathy. We grow in faith, wisdom, and understanding of painful situations. Collective mourning provides opportunities to improve our relationships with each other and those we lead. The leader who mourns identifies more closely with the people.

To lead people, we must identify with *where* they have been and *what* they are going through—before we talk about *where* we want to lead them. We acquire a deeper understanding of painful situations when we have experienced pain ourselves. We become more approachable. That is the blessing that can come through times of mourning. *It is through our own suffering that we can learn to empathize with the pain of others*, which is required of leadership.

Compassion literally means to *suffer with* another person. When we empathize closely with another person, we can really *feel* something. We experience *solidarity*, which means we lose ourselves in the struggle of another. We move from *self*-centered to *other*-centered.

Emotional Intelligence

Mourning enhances our ability to understand how emotions play a major role in interpersonal dynamics, including (1) what emotions we are feeling, (2) what emotions others are feeling, (3) how we express our own emotions, and (4) how we respond to the emotions of others.

For more on emotional intelligence, visit:

www.blessingsforleaders.com

The person who mourns nurtures emotional intelligence (EI). This is a growing field of interest for leaders. It is measured by an emotional quotient (EQ). Research indicates that EQ is even more of a predictor of leadership success than intelligence quotient (IQ).

Emotions can filter our thoughts and affect our actions. When we are angry with someone, we are more likely to close our minds to whatever the other person is saying. We lose objectivity. Our emotional filters are not allowing us to think clearly. Unless we can break through our emotional bias, our minds may be closed to new ideas the other person is suggesting.

Emotionally mature leaders understand how emotional filters are changing the thoughts in their heads and the dynamics in the room. They are keenly aware of their own emotions and those being expressed by others. They read others and adjust to the situation. They encourage honest feedback from the people around them. They self-monitor and regulate their behavior accordingly. They respond with empathy, justice, and mercy.

Listening

We grow in empathy when we listen and respond to people who are mourning. Leading with empathy, we can grow in wisdom born of collective mourning with our people.

Jesus listened to the people (Matt 15:21-28). His ability to listen amplified his response to those who mourned. To *listen from the heart*, as Jesus did, is a gift from the listener to the speaker. When we listen, we grow in empathy, show respect, and build trust.

Active listening requires maximum concentration, close attention, and full presence. An interactive process like leadership relies heavily on open, honest, and direct communication.

To really listen, we need to be able to absorb what the other person is saying. We cannot be self-absorbed with our own ideas or distracted by the noise in our world. In an increasingly narcissistic and distracted world, listening is becoming more important and less common.

Listening drills can dramatize the problems with distracted listening. When listening is attempted in crowded rooms or public places, the interruptions and distractions multiply. Both activities suffer when we try to listen while performing other tasks.

Some of my graduate students are residence hall directors. They describe situations where college roommates use email and text messages to try to resolve conflicts. They quote students as saying, "I've tried to communicate with him . . . Look, I've texted him ten times in the past two days about this." What they did *not* attempt is active listening.

My brother Billy is an information technology specialist for a glass company. He says that leadership today is hindered by cell phones and computers: "Our best leaders are the best listeners, and our interpersonal relationships are weakening through the technology age."

Information is not communication. Cell phones and computers improve access to information, but that does not necessarily mean they improve communication. Distractions from cell phones can hamper our ability to listen empathetically to a person right in front of us. When we try to have multiple conversations at the same time, listening suffers first. Traveling often, I have seen how cell phones are changing cultures around the world.

In Africa, I saw people talking on cell phones in remote villages and even in the jungle. This was shocking but I realized it had its advantages. Cell phones and computers provide the technology that allows us to share experiences across large distances. They also create more distractions from active listening and face-to-face interaction. In Benin, I saw people talking on cell phones while driving "zimmy johns," which are small motor bicycles that act as taxicabs.

In Patzcuaro, Mexico, I was walking down a dusty road with my students, visiting vegetable farms surrounded by beautiful mountains. An elderly man approached. He sauntered slowly on his horse. A large sombrero covered most of his face. It seemed we had entered a time and place apart. As he rode by, a phone rang! And that Mexican cowboy, from atop his horse, pulled a cell phone out of his pocket and answered, "Hola!"

Conclusion

Yes, the world is changing. While technology has created many opportunities to improve society, it is also creating more distractions from interpersonal interaction. With our increasing access to technology, we tend to look for technical solutions to what we call *adaptive challenges*—which require changes in our attitudes, behaviors, and mind-set (see chap. 8).

In the same way that Jesus *grew in empathy by entering the human condition*, we need to embrace our own humanity. Leaders who identify with the pain and suffering of their followers grow in empathy, show more support, and become more credible.

Times of mourning can be a blessing if we allow them to become opportunities to grow in empathy. Mourning pushes us to learn and grow as human beings. We develop new relationships. We deepen others. We begin to identify more closely with the suffering of the people whom we hope to lead. We grow in wisdom, strength, and character.

Discussion Questions (*"Blessed are those who mourn"*)

1. Think about a time when you were in mourning. How were others around you able to offer some consolation?

2. Think about a time when you were able to comfort someone when he or she suffered a painful loss. How did you offer consolation?

3. As a leader, what obstacles prevent you from offering comfort to others? What distractions prevent you from listening empathetically to others?

—— *Chapter 3* ——

Humility

Blessed are the meek, for they will inherit the earth.
—*Matthew 5:5*

The meek are strong and powerful, and they use that power with moderation, self-discipline, and restraint. When I ask my students what it means to be *meek*, the typical answers are timid, shy, quiet, introverted, withdrawn, soft, and weak. Occasionally, some will add more positive qualities like patient, kind, and humble.

In the Aramaic language used by Jesus, and in the Greek used by New Testament writers, the word "meek" describes hardworking farmers and strong yet gentle farm animals, such as horses, oxen, and cattle. The Hebrew word for "meek" describes a faithful person who has the *power of free will but chooses to follow God's will* without hesitation or resentment.

In most organizations, the meek are those who do the tough, gritty work, day in and day out. Whether leaders or followers, the meek do not seek the limelight. They are slow to anger, steady in spirit, free of bitterness, and disciplined to be gentle and nonviolent.

My mother taught me to *pray like everything is in God's hands and to work like everything is in our hands.* This is the balance we seek in the Beatitudes. The first half of her statement, praying like everything is in God's hands, requires poverty of spirit. The second half, working like everything is in our hands, requires humble dedication to a mission.

How Did Jesus Teach This?

"The greatest among you will be your servant. All who exalt themselves will be humbled, and all who humble themselves will be exalted" (Matt 23:11-12).

Jesus and Moses are both described as meek in Scripture. Yet neither is considered weak, soft, or passive. Jesus was the epitome of meekness. He resisted the temptation to rely on earthly power and coercion (Matt 4:8-10). He influenced people with love, wisdom, and mercy.

Jesus said, "Come to me, all you that are weary and are carrying heavy burdens, and I will give you rest. Take my yoke upon you, and learn from me; for I am gentle and humble in heart" (Matt 11:28-29). Jesus is strong enough to take on our heavy burdens and gentle enough to be meek.

Moses was described as meek, "more so than anyone else on the face of the earth" (Num 12:3). Moses was meek when he found the wisdom to *delegate* leadership responsibility (Exod 18:13-37). His father-in-law, Jethro, noticed that Moses was trying to do everything himself. He was wearing himself out, and he was also wearing out the people of Israel. So Jethro advised Moses to train others to spread the work around. Moses demonstrated the paradoxical combination of *strength* and *humility* when he selected, trained, and delegated responsibility to others to serve as judges with him.

The people who followed Jesus were meek. Jesus lived in an agrarian society. The people worked the land. They longed to inherit the earth and to live in the house of the Lord (Ps 27:4). They were strong and faithful, and they prayed like everything was in God's hands and worked like everything was in their hands. They relied on grace and works.

What Is the Leadership Message?

So what does this have to do with leadership? At this point, you might think that the meek would be good *followers* but not necessarily *leaders*. Let's clarify a few things:

- *Leadership* is a dance that leaders and followers perform together. Let's not reduce the role of followers to unimportance. If no one is following, it is not leadership—at least not yet. Let's appreciate the critical role that followers play in leadership. They provide the *interaction* for the work of leadership.

- We are all *followers* at some time in some context. Followers become leaders and leaders become followers. We rarely pause to reflect on how we rotate between these two roles hour to hour, day to day, situation to situation. Even the president of the United States plays the role of follower at certain moments in certain situations, perhaps at a budget briefing or in a church pew.

- The best followers have the same features as the best leaders. When my students identify the characteristics of their most admired followers, they find similar traits as they do for the most admired leaders: assertive, competent, confident, cooperative, resourceful, open-minded, motivated, passionate, creative, and so forth. Followers do *not* have to be passive, docile, or submissive.

> *Courageous followership can be the best training for leadership.*

Leaders who are meek combine the dual qualities that author Jim Collins described as "Level Five Leadership" in his book *Good to Great*. Collins described the two paradoxical qualities as (1) a "personal sense of humility" and (2) the "professional will to drive results."

Followers who are meek combine the dual qualities of (1) assertiveness and (2) cooperation that epitomize "Courageous Followership," which author Ira Chaleff has found to be critical to organizational success. Courageous followers take the initiative and work in teams.

Leaders who are meek enough to be present on the front line expand their influence. It brings them closer to the people being served, closer to the work being done. It provides insight that some people might miss, demonstrates integrity, and builds credibility.

Followers who take initiative can emerge as leaders. One of my students describes a teacher's aide who moved from follower to leader at her grade school. This woman showed up for work early every morning and greeted the students with great cheer as they came off the bus. She brought bursts of energy and enthusiasm—which is leadership!

Followers Matter

Over time, the teacher's aide changed the culture of the early morning routine at that school. Kids showed up smiling. They were more positive, cheerful, and ready to learn. No one fully appreciated the leadership role that the teacher's aide played until she was on sick leave for several weeks. The teachers who rotated in place of the teacher's aide felt obligated and coerced to do that job. They called it "bus duty." They lacked enthusiasm and it showed. Imagine the joy for students, teachers, and everyone when the teacher's aide returned to school.

Positionally, the meek can be leaders or followers. *Relationally*, the meek can emerge as leaders when they show initiative and begin to influence others. Leaders who are meek are not threatened when their followers show leadership. As the following story shows, leaders who are meek encourage their followers to be *transformed into leaders*.

John Kiley

John Kiley had a way of making everyone else around him better. As president of United Way of the Quad Cities, John was responsible for raising about $9 million per year for nonprofit organizations that serve children, families, and individuals in need.

John was *humble*. He knew that without other people around him, he could not succeed. He did not have a big personal ego that needed to be stroked with credit for his fund-raising success. He was a master at using self-deprecating humor to release tension. At United Way events, John would have fun by wearing his bright red jacket or silly ties and using that to poke fun at himself. This helped others feel comfortable around John.

Charitable fund-raising, as John realized, means you are raising money for a mission, not for yourself. Fund-raising requires *influence*. You cannot coerce, command, and control donors. You must invite, encourage, and inspire them. You must *intrinsically* motivate donors. They have the free will to choose to spend or contribute their money elsewhere.

John was a professional. He networked to promote stewardship to United Way. John was intentional about developing one-on-one relationships and personally asking for donations. He built partnerships to leverage community assets. He got to know everyone in the community. And he immediately let people know that they were important in his eyes.

John was a *team builder*. He walked around and encouraged people. He asked for suggestions for improvement. When he asked, "How you doing?" he really wanted to know. If you said "Fine," you better mean it or John would probe further to find out what was happening.

John was *competent in handling conflict.* When you talked to John, you could easily bring up conflict because he could *separate the person from the problem*. He focused on solving the problem at hand instead of looking to blame someone. John was more concerned about *what he could do* to support his team than *what they could do* to support *him*.

John's meekness made him more powerful. He used power wisely, gently, and for the benefit of his team and mission. He inspired people to give generously in service to the mission.

Credit, Blame, and Attribution

Generally speaking, leaders get more credit for team success and more blame for team failure than deserved. The wise leader recognizes this, shares the credit with others when things are going well, and shoulders the brunt of the blame when things are not going so well.

These were two of John Kiley's most effective leadership behaviors. They are what author Jim Collins identified in CEOs who took their companies from good to great:

1. Giving credit to others when things are going well. This is the *window*. The leader looks out the window, sees the followers doing well, and spreads the credit around.

2. Taking the blame when things are not going so well. This is the *mirror*. The leader looks into the mirror and squarely places the blame on himself or herself.

Giving credit came naturally for John because he was meek. When credit was due, John's instincts were to pass it around—to his staff, board, business leaders, and community volunteers. At his annual meetings, John would credit one person after another. Everyone was recognized somehow. He gave credit to the public leaders of the United Way campaign, but also to the unsung heroes that worked in the trenches and rarely received any recognition.

> *Blessed are Leaders who are Meek*

When it came to *taking the blame*, as a leader, John was willing to assume responsibility—even when the mistake was not necessarily his own. He provided cover to his staff and volunteers. For that, the loyalty of his team grew. Accountability grew. John showed how loyalty, camaraderie, and commitment to a team increase accountability to that team. His team members assumed responsibility for their mistakes because of the way that John modeled accountability.

Attribution theory suggests that as human beings, we generally are wired to attribute *external* factors to explain our failures when we make a mistake. And we attribute *internal* factors to explain why we succeed. Attribution theory works in six directions:

1. When we succeed, we tend to look to *internal* factors to glorify our achievement: "It must have been our extraordinary knowledge, skills, and abilities."

2. When we fail, we are inclined to blame an *external* factor: "The kids kept me up late last night . . . The traffic was too heavy . . . The dog ate my homework."

3. When the people we like (our in-group) succeed, we attribute *internal* factors to explain their success: "They are great people . . . They are gifted and talented."

4. When the people we like (our in-group) fail, we look to *external* factors: "They didn't get the support they needed . . . They didn't have the resources to get the job done."

5. When the people we dislike (our out-group) succeed, we attribute *external* factors: "They got lucky . . . Someone else helped them out . . . The job must have been easy."

6. When the people we dislike (our out-group) fail, we blame *internal* factors: "See, they must be lazy . . . They are unqualified . . . They just don't care enough."

John Kiley turned attribution theory on its head. He gave credit to others when things were going well and took the blame when things were not going well. He deflected praise and absorbed blame. This is practicing the *leadership wisdom of the Beatitudes.*

Leaders like John get results. Their followers work at full capacity. They contribute to the success of the team. Eventually, the followers emerge as leaders. Organizations like United Way require lots of leaders—people who are willing to take the initiative and influence others into contributing to United Way.

Meekness nurtures the wisdom to recognize that the leader does not have to be the only leader. Meekness fosters the confidence to encourage followers to challenge the leader and become leaders themselves. Meekness allows the leader to transform followers into leaders.

When John Kiley passed away in 2009, the entire community turned out to mourn the loss of this community leader. His wake and funeral were a time of relationship building (like the stories shared in chap. 2). His legacy lives on in the many leaders he developed.

Glenn Smiley

Glenn Smiley of the Fellowship of Reconciliation was a nonviolence trainer. Glenn spent five years working side by side with Martin Luther King Jr., teaching and training King and other civil rights leaders in the art, science, and philosophy of Gandhian nonviolence.

During the 1980s, I had the good fortune to spend a lot of time with Glenn. Humility was one of his key traits. One of the first things I noticed about Glenn was that he was usually the last one to speak at a meeting. When Glenn spoke at a meeting, he would summarize the points made before him, crediting others (by name) for their ideas, reflecting on how their ideas inspired him, distinguishing what he agreed with and what he disagreed with, and drawing conclusions based on what others had said. This approach had a powerful impact on me.

> *The key to effective leadership is dynamic listening.*

Glenn's practice of *letting others speak first* and then summarizing points of agreement and disagreement are critical to the process called the *five-step meeting*. It is part of a course titled Leadership through People Skills, which I teach at St. Ambrose University. It is designed for one-on-one meetings but can be adapted to team meetings as well:

1. *Establish the purpose* and set the agenda for the meeting. Make sure the other person is receptive to holding the meeting at this time.

2. *Listen.* Let the other person speak to the issue while you demonstrate that you understand what is being said and can relate to the emotions being expressed.

3. *Present your views.* Explain what you agree with and what you disagree with. Be assertive about your own needs and interests.

4. *Resolve your differences.* Work through each dimension of the problem. Remain assertive while also being cooperative with the other person's needs and interests.

5. *Solidify the agreement* and clarify the next steps. Meetings that skip this step are destined to be repeated.

For more on the five-step meeting, visit:

www.blessingsforleaders.com

In each step of this five-step meeting, summarize what you hear. To summarize is to put what the other person said into your words and to check for understanding. It is amazing how many issues can be resolved with this simple method. Summarizing does not mean agreement! It signifies understanding. It builds your credibility and your relationship with the other person. It is an efficient use of time because you get the message right the first time.

Listening can be persuasive. If you listen carefully to the ideas of others, they will be more likely to listen to your ideas. To build consensus around a solution, a la Glenn Smiley, focus your attention on what is being said, rather than rehearsing what to say.

Conclusion

The best followers become leaders. The best leaders develop their followers into leaders. Followership can be the best training for leadership: if we want to become great leaders, we must first be courageous followers, those who take initiative.

Meek leaders lead others to lead themselves. The meek are humble enough to rely on great followers and prepare them to be great leaders. They encourage their followers to step up. They remain open to new ideas and welcome critical feedback. They gain power, not for power's sake, but for the sake of the team, the organization, and the mission. They share power.

Leaders who are meek involve their followers in the process of making decisions, solving problems, and addressing challenges. They influence without coercion. They model how to be both cooperative and assertive. They encourage their followers to be cooperative and assertive. They recognize that leadership is a *voluntary* relationship that models God's ways by providing free will to the people being led.

Discussion Questions (*"Blessed are the meek"*)

1. Name some strong leaders whom you would describe as meek.

2. As a leader, how well do you share the credit with others when you succeed?

3. As a leader, how well do you accept the blame when you fail?

Chapter 4

Justice

Blessed are those who hunger and thirst for righteousness, for they will be filled.
—Matthew 5:6

To be *right* about something usually means it is just, moral, true, or correct. To be *right with God* is to discern the will of God and surrender your free will to God's will.

To be *just* is to *treat people right* in the collective sense of the word. When we say that we "treated someone right," we usually mean that we were just, fair, honest, and sincere.

The words *right and just* are often used interchangeably. They are used to define each other. The distinctions are very subtle. According to St. Thomas Aquinas, being *right* means giving to God what God is due and being *just* is giving people what the people are due (ST II–II, q. 57, a. 1).

In this Beatitude, to be *righteous* is to combine the two—to be *right and just*. To say something is "right and just" means that it is right with God and just with the people.

To be *right in relationship with God* requires that we are *just in relationship to others*. In the Aramaic language that Jesus used, righteousness is a holistic concept that incorporates justice, mercy, and faithfulness. The righteous are just, merciful, and faithful.

Hunger for righteousness begins with a right relationship with God. The righteous prioritize their relationships with God, family, friends, colleagues, and community. To hunger for a right relationship with God is to be poor in spirit.

Hunger for righteousness extends to the people on our teams and in our organizations. We cannot be in right relationship with God if we are not building right relationships in our families and communities and in society itself. The righteous strive for relationships that are healthy, agreements that are fair, and systems that are just.

Hunger instills and enhances motivation. Athletes excel when they are hungry for victory. They can outperform and upset those who have more talent but are overly confident. Victory can reduce hunger. When satisfied, we lose our competitive edge. Teams that are hungry play their hearts out. Hunger is a motivating factor. Team leaders create a sense of hunger for victory in order to motivate their teams.

The righteous are keenly aware of the need for justice. They hunger for a sense of purpose and direction. That hunger becomes a deep longing in their hearts. They long for a renewed sense of justice in the community around them. They act with integrity.

How Did Jesus Teach This?

"Thus says the LORD: Act with justice and righteousness"
(Jer 22:3).

The Beatitudes are autobiographical depictions of the traits and behaviors of Jesus. Jesus was poor in spirit. He mourned, he was meek, and he hungered for righteousness.

Jesus prepared for his public ministry by fasting (Matt 4:1-11). Fasting intensifies hunger. Fasting is an intentional way to create a void. Jesus wanted to create a vacuum that could only be filled with God's presence. Doing the will of God was his food (Matt 4:4). Jesus fasted to create a greater hunger for righteousness.

This Beatitude teaches that those who hunger for righteousness will be filled now. Righteousness is a sign of the kingdom "on earth as it is in heaven" (Matt 6:9-13). It signifies a time of right relationships. People are living right with God and acting just with each other.

The story of the Last Judgment teaches that *the righteous*—those who have fed the hungry, given drink to the thirsty, clothed the naked, welcomed the immigrants, comforted the sick, and visited the imprisoned—will be welcomed into the kingdom of heaven (Matt 25:31-46). The virtuous works of the Beatitudes are all there.

Jesus teaches that those who hunger for right relationships will be *blessed now* and those who practice righteousness will be *welcomed into eternal life*. The hunger for righteousness will be filled now *and* for eternity.

Jesus teaches that relationships are more important than rules.

The scribes and the Pharisees were self-righteous. They focused on rules and regulations to make sure things were done "their way," not necessarily the "right way." They jockeyed for position, promotion, and publicity. They cared only for selfish interests instead of caring for the people they were supposed to lead.

Relationship-Based Business

Beatitudes leaders are right and just. They give God what is due and in so doing, they give people what they are due. They build right relationships. In the first chapter, we focused on right relationships with God. Let's take a closer look at how leaders build right relationships with their followers.

When leaders take care of their workers, the workers are more likely to take care of the customers. This is especially true with workers on the front line. Customers will be treated well because the frontline workers have the most direct contact with the customers. Satisfied customers become repeat customers. They can be the lifeline of many businesses.

Retail business was not always as impersonal and hypercompetitive as it is today. My father Bob Ebener was a furniture salesman for over forty years. His business was based on *relationships*. He sold furniture at a locally owned business in a small community. He worked at a time when your word, your honor, and your handshake meant everything. His customers did not shop around for the best price before buying furniture. They made one stop and that was to see my father. His customers shopped at his store based not on price but on *relationship*.

Customers were friends and neighbors, not nameless shoppers hunting for the lowest price. If something broke, my father's store fixed it. If the customer came back unsatisfied with the deal, my father listened and met their needs. By the time he retired, the whole furniture business was going through major upheavals due to competition from large corporate businesses. Customers were beginning to shop around and make purchases based on the lowest price.

Customer Service

We can learn a lot about business by looking at how retail worked during my father's time. Knowing your customer's name was important. My father knew everyone in town. Serving your customer was important. Customers were people you cared about. Customer service was more than a company slogan: you lived it. Professional reputation meant everything. Acting with integrity was critical for every transaction. Your relationship with the customer was your future business. Customer service gave my father a sense of *purpose*.

Serving the community was a core value. My father built relationships with friends, neighbors, customers, and other business leaders. He used that network to lead community efforts to build a Little League diamond, a swimming pool, and tennis courts in our small town of Oglesby, Illinois. He donated his time, talent, and treasure. Then he asked others, especially other business leaders, to join him. That was his way of giving back to the community.

Clydesdale's

While my father was not the owner of his furniture business, he had a sense of ownership because the owners treated him like

Blessed are Leaders who Hunger for Righteousness

an owner. When I was hospitalized at seven months old with spinal meningitis, my parents did not have health insurance. Seventeen days in a hospital must have cost a fortune, even in 1954. When I recovered with a miraculous cure, John Clydesdale, who owned the furniture business where my father worked, asked my father for the hospital bill. He told my father, "Don't worry about it. I've got this covered." Can you imagine that happening today?

The Clydesdales knew that my father would be more intrinsically motivated if he felt a sense of ownership about their family business. So they treated him like family. My father extended that kindness to the customers. This was a *relationship-based* approach to business, something that worked for my father, for the Clydesdales, and for the customer. While it may be less common today, it continues to be an effective approach.

What Is the Leadership Message?

Which is more important: Getting the job done *or* making the people happy? This is a false dichotomy because it poses an either/or question when the answer is *both*. Leaders do both: they are in right relationship *and* they are dedicated to mission, vision, and goals.

Leaders are effective when they succeed on both the task and the relationship.

Building positive relationships on your team increases the likelihood that you will get the job done. And vice versa. The two go together. A cohesive team usually gets better results. Achieving your goals usually builds stronger bonds on the team. People who are bonded by a common mission and inspired by a shared vision are more likely to get the job done. Relationships can be improved by a leader who is thoughtful, supportive, and collaborative.

Leadership and Trust

Trust is critical to right relationships. We build trust, gain credibility, and develop character by practicing virtuous behaviors that are *righteous*.

Trust is the grease that keeps an organization working smoothly. When people trust the leader, and the leader trusts the people, the work goes more smoothly. Without trust, people become more suspicious of each other and are less loyal to the organization.

> *Trust is both the glue and the grease that make things happen in organizational life.*

Trust is the glue that holds an organization together. When trust breaks down, everything can fall apart. This is particularly true when the work requires more interdependence between the leader and followers.

Trust is a key ingredient to social capital, which is the net social relationships on a team or in an organization. It is *right relationships* at the organizational level. Social capital can be measured as the *trust* between workers and management, *camaraderie* among the workers, *commitment* of the people to the mission, and *loyalty* of the workers to the organization.

The more we collaborate, the more trust will grow. The more we trust, the more we will be able to collaborate. Trust and collaboration have a powerful effect on each other.

So how do we develop trust? Do we develop trust by trusting others? Not really. The best way to build trust is to *be trustworthy*. We cannot completely control whether the other party is going to be trustworthy. We build trust by being *right and just*.

One of the greatest mistakes I made as a young manager was thinking I could create trust by trusting others. Trust begins with small steps and when the other party responds in a trustworthy manner, more trust is offered. Trust is built slowly, gradually, and carefully.

Trust is a five-way street. It works in five directions. Each is related to *confidence*. The word "confidence" is based on the Latin root *fides*, which means "faith" or "belief." When we *believe* in all five of the following directions, trust can be developed:

1. The self-confidence of the leader

2. The confidence of the leader in the followers

3. The self-confidence of the followers

4. The confidence of the followers in each other

5. The confidence of the followers in the leader

Confidence and *competence* have a reciprocal effect on each other. As one grows, the other grows as well. *Confidence is being willing.* It is the belief we have in ourselves or others. *Competence is being able.* It is the skill we develop for a particular job. Confidence grows out of developing the knowledge, skills, and abilities necessary for a certain position. If a person wants and needs to grow in self-confidence, then developing the necessary skills for that job is the first step. *As we grow in competence, our confidence will grow.* And vice versa.

Trust: A Five-Way Street
To build trust, follow these steps:

1. *Believe in yourself.* Develop your skills and you will grow in self-confidence.

2. *Believe in your people.* Develop skills specific to the task that needs to be done. As you believe in them, they are more likely to believe in themselves.

3. *Encourage the people to believe in themselves.* As people improve their skills, they will also become more self-confident.

4. *Encourage the people to believe in each other.* As skills improve, the people will learn to rely on each other. They will form trust.

5. *Demonstrate that the people can believe in you as their leader.* Practice what you preach. Do what you say. Live with *integrity*. Integrate your *core values* with your actions. Be *right and just*. This is the essence of *right relationships*.

Integrity is the most fundamental trait for leaders—and followers. Lack of integrity by either party can cause delay, departure, or division in the buildup of trust. Integrity is the foundation upon which we can establish *just systems* and *right relationships*.

> *Integrity Matters*

Core Values

Core values are critical to right relationships. When leaders act consistently on core values, they build trust and develop right relationships. Imagine a company that says customer service is a core value. Customers will pick up on the integrity of that claim by asking:

- How am I treated when I call customer service?

- How am I treated when I walk into a store?

- How do the behaviors of the workers fit the core values of the organization?

Core values are an integral part of organizational culture. Culture is reflected by attitudes, beliefs, norms, and, most important, the way people do things.

> *Culture does change. To change the culture, we must first change the behaviors.*

We are more likely to act ourselves into a new way of thinking than to think ourselves into a new way of acting. Leaders change thinking by changing what people are doing.

The mother of a Vietnamese friend taught that "every grain of rice is a gift from God." This is a value that runs counter to the common belief that we are entitled to things. To embed this value into our culture would require changing attitudes and beliefs about food. Leaders could start such a cultural change by first changing some wasteful behaviors.

Leaders change culture. Culture is hard to change and is generally the last thing to change in a change process. When I consult with organizations, I set up a process to help them identify and articulate their core values. Then I suggest they hire people who are already committed to those values. The core values can be used to design interviewing questions to see if new applicants would fit the culture. It is harder to change people's values after they are hired.

For more on core values, visit:

www.blessingsforleaders.com

The *core values process* that I developed with John Kiley for United Way gets people talking about their core values. For example, CEO Diane Nelson of the Girl Scouts and I visited several cities in Iowa for core values workshops. Hundreds of girls, parents, and friends of the Girl Scouts gathered to identify and articulate values, such as relationships, character, empowerment, and service. The most powerful experience was when the Girl Scouts themselves stood up and spoke in their own words about what these values meant to them.

Conclusion

To be righteous is to build right relationships and just systems. This is the basis for developing trust, commitment, and cohesiveness on our teams and in our organizations. If leaders serve the workers, the workers will serve the customers. If leaders treat the people right, the people will treat the customers right. Establishing right relationships is critical to completing the mission, getting the job done, and reaching organizational goals (the *task* of leadership).

Leaders build community and establish culture by stating core values and by practicing behaviors consistent with the culture they want to create: They practice what they preach. They set a consistent example. They act *right with God* and *just with others*. Leaders develop *integrity* by *integrating* their behaviors with their core values. They do what they say and say what they do.

Discussion Questions
(*"Blessed are those who hunger and thirst for righteousness"*)

1. What are your core values in life?

2. What are the core values of the organization you lead? How well do your core values line up with those of the organization you lead?

3. As a leader, how do you monitor your own integrity? How do you make sure that you practice integrity by integrating your values and behaviors?

Chapter 5

Mercy

Blessed are the merciful, for they will receive mercy.
—*Matthew 5:7*

M ercy is empathy in action. Empathy sees a need and mercy
fills it. To act with mercy is to rescue the lowly, comfort
the afflicted, and reduce the misery in our neighbor's life.
Mercy restores a sense of righteousness. Mercy forgives transgressions and corrects injustice. It is unconditional. Mercy is the
healthy approach whether we think the other person deserves it
or not. Mercy reconciles relationships so we can be returned to
wholeness.

Mercy demands a change in the system. Mercy starts with charity and provides direct assistance. But it does not stop there. Mercy
goes beyond the demands of charity, the letter of the law, and the
requirements of civil discourse. Mercy demands *justice*.

The corporal works of mercy are based on Matthew 25:31-46.
They are to feed the hungry, give drink to the thirsty, clothe the naked,
offer hospitality to the homeless, visit the prisoner, care for the sick,
and bury the dead. Jesus describes this as the work of the *righteous*.

The spiritual works of mercy provide for the spirit what the corporal works of mercy provide for the body. They are to instruct the uninformed, counsel the doubtful, admonish sinners, bear wrongs patiently, forgive offenses willingly, comfort the afflicted, and pray for the living, the sick, and the dead. They encourage *poverty of spirit.*

How Did Jesus Teach This?

The righteous show mercy (see Ps 37:21).

According to Jesus, the basis of mercy is *love.* Love of God and neighbor is the Great Commandment (Matt 22:37-40). When the sheep are placed on the right side in the story of the Last Judgment, Jesus calls them the *righteous.* The righteous act with love. They perform the *works of mercy*: they feed the hungry and shelter the homeless (Matt 25:31-46).

When Jesus teaches the Our Father (Matt 6:9-13), he provides a script to pray by the Beatitudes. Jesus prays, "And forgive us our debts, as we also have forgiven our debtors" (Matt 6:12). His first comment after teaching the Our Father reminds us that we will only be forgiven if we are merciful and forgive others their transgressions (Matt 6:14).

Jesus says that *justice, mercy,* and *faithfulness* are the more important matters of the law that are neglected by the legalists (Matt 23:23). In Matthew 23, Jesus criticizes the scribes and Pharisees in the fiercest language: he calls them "blind guides" (Matt 23:16), "blind fools" (Matt 23:17), and "hypocrites" (Matt 23:27). They understand *the letter* but do not practice *the spirit* of the law—*mercy based on love.*

What Is the Leadership Message?

Mercy creates the opportunity for followers to be fully engaged, to innovate, to be resourceful, and to partner with others for new, collaborative ideas for change.

Wisdom teaches us humility about our shortcomings. We learn to acknowledge what we do not know and to admit to ourselves and others what we need to know. Partial knowledge can be very dangerous, especially when we pretend to have all the right answers.

Leaders are expected to have all the answers. If we think we have all the answers, we are not really poor in spirit. We don't really need followers. We are not open to new ideas, and we fail to ask the right questions. When leaders walk around, see what is happening, and ask people what they think, they find new and creative solutions to persistent problems.

Merciful leaders get honest answers. They see the true picture of what is happening because the people will be less fearful about sharing their ideas and experiences. Research shows that the best ideas emerge from team meetings with high levels of *task conflict*, which occurs when we have differences of opinion about the subject matter or the job itself, but low levels of *relationship conflict*, which occurs when we have people problems.

The best innovators are often found on the ground floor. These change agents need support from the top floor. The middle floor (middle management) is often the bottleneck. Midlevel managers tend to be the most resistant to change. Generally speaking, managers tend to promote order and avoid risks. Bureaucracy is designed to *cover* risks, not to expose the organization to new risks. Leaders need to encourage managers to be open to new ideas.

Blessed are Leaders who Show Mercy

Leaders need to be prudent in taking risks. They encourage and empower people to take sensible risks—not just to change for the sake of change. Followers need to know that the leader is merciful. The leader who shows "no mercy" will stifle creativity and generate fear of failure.

Managers can stifle innovation when they try to control everything. Micromanagement is the extreme example of control. It can indicate a lack of trust and discourages creative thinking. It wastes time, energy, and ideas that can come from the ground floor.

Merciful Leaders

The Lord is kind and merciful (see Ps 103:8).

Can leaders be kind *and* merciful? Can leaders be helpful, thoughtful, and merciful without being weak or soft? Can leaders be accountable *and* merciful?

Mercy applies to both the *task* and the *relationship* of leadership. Merciful leaders promote accountability on the task and understanding on the relationship *at the same time.*

To be merciful on the task means to interpret everyday tasks as part of the mission and then to hold people accountable for that mission. Merciful leaders recognize how the *works of mercy* are associated with the mission. This includes both the spiritual and corporal works of mercy, such as feeding, sheltering, clothing, caring, teaching, counseling, or comforting.

Merciful leaders delve deeper into the mission. They explain how the daily tasks of the people provide a social benefit that goes *beyond and below the bottom line* of profitability.

To be merciful on the relationship side of leadership is to allow space for the people to make mistakes. Merciful leaders are supportive, cooperative, and thoughtful.

Remember that to measure leadership as either task *or* relationship is to succumb to a false dichotomy. Leadership metrics generally fall into two categories: (1) Is the job getting done? (2) Are the people happy? The first is the *task*; the second is the *relationship*.

Authors Robert Blake and Jane Mouton suggest that the most effective leader is *assertive* on the task and *cooperative* on the relationship at the same time. The job gets done and the needs of the people are fulfilled. The people are resourceful and collaborative.

A "leader" who is supportive on the relationship side of leadership but is not getting the job done is weak. People come to socialize but there is no accountability for getting things done. This leader may lack passion for the mission or clarity about the vision. Or perhaps this leader just wants to be liked by everyone. Paradoxically, the people will not even like this leader if the people are truly dedicated to the mission. If the vision is a shared vision, the people will want to see progress toward that vision. Dedicated followers want to see results.

Leaders can be both accountable on the task and merciful on the relationship.

A "leader" who is assertive on the task (getting the job done) but is not supportive on the relationship is not effective either. Research shows that this approach can work for short periods of time, such as in emergencies. According to authors Paul Hersey and Ken Blanchard, a directive style can be brutal when the work is repetitive or the workers already know the job. Most people will leave, resist, or rebel against a workplace dictator. If they have a choice in the matter, they will find another line of work or a different team.

Leaders need to be accountable on the task and supportive on the relationship at the same time. In other words, leaders need to be passionate about the merciful work of the mission *and* helpful, thoughtful, and merciful in the way they build relationships on the team. This style of leadership is a *quantum leap* for most people who see assertiveness on the task and cooperation on the relationship as mutually exclusive!

Leaders Who Succeed on the Task and Relationship

Linda Frederiksen and Kevin Greenley of MEDIC use the latest technology to save lives with emergency medical services (EMS). They are driven by their core value of compassion, which they describe this way: "Personified in everything we do for those we care for and work alongside." Integrity is "embedded in our core, developed through our actions." Linda and Kevin practice what they preach: they take time to respond to emergency calls and ride with their EMS workers. The workers show loyalty for their leaders, build camaraderie with their colleagues, and demonstrate commitment to the mission of MEDIC.

Julie Martens and Clyde Mayfield have a head for business and a heart for the world. They are committed to their mission to provide healthy food and a wholesome atmosphere at their natural food store, Greatest Grains on Earth. This local grocery store and deli has become a meeting place for neighbors, students, and community leaders who gather for a healthy dose of food and the company of strangers who become friends at this unique business. Clyde serves as a leader with many community organizations and volunteers as a mentor and coach for kids. He and Julie serve as role models for people in their low-income neighborhood.

Sharon DeFrieze, a volunteer leader with Christian Care, is committed to their mission: "To transform lives by serving the least, the last and the lost." She bridges the gap between staff and board by volunteering regularly at the domestic violence shelter, raising money for the rescue mission, and providing stability to their board of directors.

Marty Kurtz, Eric Kies, and Matthew Sivertsen of The Planning Center are passionate about their mission: "In a complex financial world filled with unknowns, we provide objectivity and clarity to create peace of mind." Marty is founder of the financial planning firm but has no hesitation in delegating responsibilities to his young protégés, Eric and Matt. They pay attention to the relational side of the business by starting staff meetings with a "check-in" to see how everyone is doing before jumping into business. They conclude meetings with a "check-out," asking for a high point of the meeting and making sure everyone is on the same page as the meeting adjourns. This also creates a starting point for the next meeting.

Cheryl Goodwin, as CEO of Family Resources, Inc. (FRI), is passionate about their mission: "To strengthen children, families and individuals by providing quality services that engage community resources to create effective solutions." Her legacy at FRI will be her devotion to building relationships. She goes out of her way to make her presence visible to the agency staff of 380 social workers, educators, and support people.

Ian Frink and Jim Maynard, as vice presidents and co-owners of Crawford Company, are loyal to their core values of teamwork, innovation, quality, and customer service. They are building a strong culture around those core values and increased commitment to the values by involving all eighty-plus employees of their heating and air-conditioning business in a process to identify and articulate these core values and to put them into practice (see chap. 8).

Bishop Martin Amos and Msgr. John Hyland, as leaders of the Diocese of Davenport, build relationships on their team by practicing participative leadership. They invite their staff to co-create the agenda for all directors meetings. They are faithful to their mission: "Go and make disciples of all nations to love God and neighbor" (based on Matt 28:19), and to their vision: "To reflect the kingdom of God by growing in faith, hope and charity."

Anne Armknecht and Chris McCormick Pries view their mission at Vera French Community Mental Health Center as "empowering people to develop strengths and instill hope." They demonstrated their belief in empowerment by involving their staff in the core values workshops and focus groups as part of their strategic planning process.

Jim Tiedje, a volunteer leader with Café on Vine, devotes himself to this mission: "To promote human dignity by providing food for the hungry and advocating for an end to hunger." When founder Father Marv Mottet retired as board chair, Jim stepped up to assume that role. He coordinates the active engagement of a team of volunteers who serve on the board.

Leslie Kilgannon, a community organizer for Quad Cities Interfaith, states her mission as "empowering ordinary people to effectively participate." She supports, encourages, and develops leaders such as Loxi Hopkins and Nora Dvorak, who lead as volunteers.

Intrinsic Motivation

Leaders who are both passionate about the mission of the organization and dedicated to the people on their teams increase *intrinsic* motivation for the followers. This is the essence of what author Bernard Bass calls *transformational leadership*. It augments *transactional leadership*, which provides extrinsic rewards that are necessary but not sufficient.

Followers who are intrinsically motivated are more dedicated to their work. They perform above and beyond the call of duty. They help others, participate in organizational activities, cheerlead for the organization, take initiative, and take personal responsibility to continuously self-develop their skills and talents.

Innovation

Command and control tactics stifle creativity. Fear tactics discourage innovation. When a team goes out on a limb, tries something new, and then fails, they can be devastated. They need accountability but not the humiliation of someone with positional authority accusing, blaming, and punishing them for their mistakes.

New ideas can come from new people who bring a fresh perspective. A generous donor at St. Ambrose University, where I teach, was visiting campus for the first time in a long time. His hosts were eager to make a positive impression. After a tour of the campus,

Ideas Matter

he said he was truly amazed at the physical growth and aesthetic changes. But his first impression was something that his hosts had seen hundreds of times but no longer noticed. Apparently, there was a dumpster outside the cafeteria where they had started his tour. It's amazing how a new set of eyes can see things the rest of us take for granted.

Some of the best ideas come from people at the grassroots, if the leader can encourage people to share those ideas. For twenty years, I supervised a Catholic Charities program that offered immigration counseling services. The Latina women who worked in that office considered me *el Jefe*, which is Spanish for "the Boss." It took years to break them of their cultural inclination to defer to me for decisions they could make themselves or problems they could solve themselves.

I had to develop new habits of my own—and practice the five-step meeting process (see chap. 3). For example, when they approached me with a problem, I would ask, "So what do you think we should do about that?" Usually, the person bringing you the problem already has a solution in mind. In fact, they may have been pondering it for days or weeks.

The key to the five-step meeting process is to listen before you speak. Summarize their ideas and test for understanding. Present your ideas in terms of what you agree with and what you might disagree with from their ideas. Then work out the differences.

My immigration staff knew their business much better than I did. They just needed me to facilitate a process to build consensus around their ideas and solutions. We often feel an obligation as leaders to fix the problem ourselves and we make the mistake of going first with our suggested solutions. What I learned was that my immigration staff usually had better ideas than mine anyway. Going second spared me the humiliation of sharing my weaker ideas at all.

My colleague Randy Richards has an ingenious approach to solving problems. He makes *solving the other person's problem his problem.* Randy uses a Socratic method of asking the right questions to elicit the right thinking around a problem. He is relentless about probing until finding a solution that suits everyone's interests.

Randy also suggests that organizations change the style of their meetings. Leaders should hold more meetings to *problem solve* instead of meetings to persuade or to inform. Meetings should be held to *generate new ideas*, to explore their usefulness in *solving problems*, and to *discern the wisdom* of the group.

In meetings to *persuade*, the decisions have already been made. Someone is calling a meeting to convince everyone else to go along. These meetings sometimes make a sham of integrity by feigning open-mindedness when clearly something has already been decided.

In meetings to *inform*, someone calls a meeting to inform people of what has already been decided. There are no pretentions of persuasion. Meetings to inform or persuade are common to board meetings, staff meetings, and most organizational meetings.

In meetings to *problem solve*, we demonstrate leadership. Instead of holding meetings to inform our people about decisions we already made, or meetings to persuade them to support our ideas, leaders facilitate an interactive process to solve a present, future, or recurring problem.

For more on team meetings, visit:

WWW

www.blessingsforleaders.com

Conclusion

Leaders who are merciful on both the task and the relationship are in the best position to bring about change. They tie the tasks of the organization to the spiritual and corporal works of mercy. They bring a missionary zeal to the everyday work the people do.

Merciful leaders create a merciful culture that promotes learning and reduces fear of change. They give people the space to experiment with new ideas and possibly to make mistakes. They rid themselves of the positional mentality that can destroy relationships, and they have the humility to admit they need the people and their ideas. They build trust, demonstrate openness to new ideas, and yet insist on accountability. The people become more resourceful and collaborative.

Merciful leaders are willing to put unsolved problems squarely on the table. They search for new ideas, listen for understanding, value everyone's opinions, stimulate differences of opinion, and seek collaborative solutions. They create synergy on their teams and discover new, bold solutions that are more effective than any individual could create.

Discussion Questions (*"Blessed are the merciful"*)

1. How can you reinterpret the work of your organization as doing the works of mercy, that is, feeding, sheltering, clothing, caring, teaching, counseling, or comforting others?

2. To what extent are the meetings you attend meetings to inform, meetings to persuade, or meetings to problem solve? What about the meetings you lead?

3. As a leader, how can you change the meetings you lead so you spend more time solving real problems?

—— *Chapter 6* ——

Service

Blessed are the pure in heart, for they will see God.
—*Matthew 5:8*

To be *pure of heart* means that our motives are pure and our intentions are true. Our hearts are free of ulterior motives or selfish intentions. Our goals are clear-cut and our purpose is meaningful. Our policies are fair and systems are just. Our actions are virtuous. We are free to serve God and others with all the joy and blessings that come from giving fully of ourselves.

Striving to be pure of heart is a continuous process, an ongoing quest. Like other Beatitudinal qualities, purity of heart is worth striving toward but the search is never complete. Once we think we have achieved it, it is time to reexamine our motives, goals, and actions.

The pure of heart are *single-hearted* in their service to a worthy cause. The single-hearted understand their mission in life. They are fully devoted to that mission. The single-hearted are not distracted by status or possessions. The *multi-hearted* are distracted, confused, and pulled in many directions. They lack the singular focus of a true sense of mission.

The single-hearted can "see God" because they see God's handi-work in the world around them. As author Susan Annette Muto points out, they see with *eyes of love.* They see and experience God's love in the people around them and in the beauty of creation. They keep constant attention on God through prayer, reflection, and acts of charity, justice, and mercy.

How Did Jesus Teach This?

"So the last will be first, and the first will be last" (Matt 20:16).

The Sermon on the Mount speaks to developing the heart. The religious leaders that Jesus encountered were intent on enforcing the local rituals and customs. They had veered away from the original purpose of the law. Jesus urged his disciples to pay close attention to matters of the heart and less attention to technical compliance with rules and regulations (Matt 22:34-40).

> *Purifying the heart is the interior work that Jesus prescribes.*

Jesus places the priority on the inward journey—the spirit, the heart, the mind, and the development of character. Repeatedly, Jesus cautioned his disciples against using the legalistic lens of the scribes and the Pharisees (Matt 23). They were meticulous in their at-tention to ceremonial rules, obsessive in their focus on ritual purity, and self-serving in their selection of which rules and laws to closely adhere to. Close adherence to the law distracted them from the more urgent and important interior work of *cleaning the heart.*

When the legalists tried to corner Jesus with the question of which commandment is the greatest, Jesus reframed the question and came up with a clear and memorable answer: *love is the Great Commandment*—(1) to *love God with all your heart, soul, and mind* and (2) to *love your neighbor as yourself* (Matt 22:37-39). While the scribes and Pharisees were looking for a legal answer, they got an interpretation of Scripture that speaks to the very *heart and spirit* of their religion, not the *letter* of the law.

What Is the Leadership Message?

Jesus was training his disciples for leadership by forming the heart. He taught his disciples that the inward journey of building character is vital to the success of the leader and the organization. He was preparing them for a new type of leadership that we now call *servant leadership*, a term that was framed by a Quaker named Robert Greenleaf in 1970 and a philosophy that can be traced back to the message of Jesus, Lao Tsu, and Confucius.

Servant leadership is a paradoxical philosophy. The paradoxes of servant leadership can be understood from a careful reflection on the Beatitudes, especially this one. Servant leaders prioritize the needs and interests of others and the organization ahead of their own. To the extent they are driven by service to a mission, their motives are pure and clean.

Intentions Matter

Servant leaders are motivated primarily to serve and then to lead. The motivation to serve reflects purity of heart. Leaders step *back* and develop a pure desire to serve. Servants step *up* when they want to see a change, and they decide to lead.

Servant leaders realize that, like Jesus, they are "not to be served but to serve" (Matt 20:28). When the apostles James and John approach Jesus about sitting on his right and his left when he comes in glory, Jesus reflects on leadership. He observes the Romans and how they "lord it over them," and he warns his disciples, "It will not be so among you" (Matt 20:26-27).

Whoever wishes to be great among you must be your servant, Jesus says (Matt 20:27). If you want to lead like Jesus, lead as a servant. Be a servant leader.

Seven Myths and Paradoxes about Servant Leadership

Servant leadership may seem paradoxical, but that is precisely what we would expect from a leadership style modeled by Jesus.

The servant leader is more interested in *giving* than *receiving* (Matt 5:40-42). The servant leader feels *indebted*, not *entitled*. The servant leader is a *steward* who wants to *give back* to God, to family, to community, and to others.

Pedestal "leaders" command the people and control what the people do. Pedestal "leaders" might call themselves "public servants" but they act like they are interested in serving only themselves. They seek power for the sake of power, not for the sake of the group. They lack the humility to understand that *leaders need the people as much as the people need the leaders.* In fact, they are not "leaders" at all. They are coercing, not influencing. They are practicing commandership, not leadership.

The Beatitudes provide a reflection guide for servant leaders. We are to be faithful, compassionate, humble, passionate about justice, merciful, pure of heart, peaceful, and courageous in the face of adversity (Matt 5:3-12).

In the same way that the Beatitudes and parables of Jesus reveal a sense of paradox, servant leadership—the leadership style of Jesus—is full of paradox. Let's look at seven of these paradoxes and seven myths that go with them.

Myth 1: Servant leadership is soft. When author Jim Collins was presenting the leadership style of his *Good to Great* companies, he wanted to describe them as *servant leaders.* But his research team convinced him that this term was too soft.

The paradox: Servant leadership is neither hard nor soft. There is nothing *soft* about dealing with *complex* human interaction and organizational chaos. Once the servant decides to lead, all that we know about leadership comes into play. Servant leaders address adaptive challenges, resolve conflict collaboratively, enhance communication, invite people to participate, build synergistic teams, plan strategically, and develop the leadership potential in others.

Servant leadership is not hard to understand. It is quite simple: like Jesus, the servant leader nurtures a kind and gentle heart that guides decisions and actions (Matt 6:19-24). Servant leaders put the welfare of others ahead of their own (Matt 7:12).

Myth 2: Servant leaders cannot hold positions of authority. Some people believe that powerful positions will automatically corrupt a person who wants to lead.

The paradox: Servant leadership is not a position, but people in positions can be servant leaders. Servant leadership is *relational*, not *positional*. It can emerge from anyone, anywhere. The servant leader is interested in coaching, mentoring, facilitating, and developing people into leaders. Servant leadership can be practiced with or without a position of authority. Servant leaders rotate between the roles of leadership, management, and followership.

Myth 3: Servant leaders convince people to follow their vision of the future. When a leader is appointed to a new position, some people expect the leader to articulate a new vision.

The paradox: Servant leaders create a sense of shared vision with the people they lead. The servant leaders and the people are co-creators and co-owners of that vision. Leadership is a multi-directional process that is primarily about dialogue. How we listen can be more important than what we say. The paradox of listening is that people who listen well can be very persuasive.

Myth 4: Servant leaders are selfless. Some people believe that in order to truly serve others a person must totally reject self-interest in order to overcome selfishness.

The paradox: The servant leader is humble, not selfless. Humility is not selflessness. Like all Aristotelian virtues, humility is a healthy middle ground. It is neither *selfish* nor *selfless*. Servant leaders are assertive about their own needs and interests *and* cooperative on the needs and interests of others.

Myth 5: Servant leaders do not get great results. Some people believe that servant leadership cannot work in the real world.

The paradox: Servant leaders are ambitious but direct their ambition toward the mission, not themselves. Jesus did not admonish his disciples for striving for great results. He taught them that greatness is measured by service (Matt 20:20-28). The Greenleaf

Center for Servant Leadership identifies and supports many successful businesses that practice servant leadership by putting people and purpose ahead of profits—and become even more profitable.

Myth 6: Servant leaders are powerless. Some people see all earthly power as evil. Earthly power was one of the temptations that Jesus resisted in the desert (Matt 4:8-10).

The paradox: Servant leaders gain power as they serve others. Power is simply the ability to act. Action is necessary for leadership. Power can be used for good or for evil, depending on the leader. Servant leaders expand, extend, and share the power generated by leadership. They *socialize* the power so that it increases for everyone.

Myth 7: Servant leaders "do to others as you would have them do to you" (Matt 7:12). These words, known as the Golden Rule, are familiar to virtually every religious tradition.

The paradox: Servant leaders practice the Platinum Rule and the Iron Rule. The Platinum Rule suggests that we "do unto others what *they* would have us do unto *them*." A leader listens to the people and considers what they want and need before making decisions or choosing rewards. For example, a reward that the leader might find motivating may not be the same reward that motivates all the people.

The Golden Rule should be tempered by the Iron Rule, which suggests, "Do *not* do unto others what they can do for themselves." As servant leaders, we delegate responsibilities, and then provide support and specific feedback. We give credit to God and to the people rather than being the Teflon leader who deflects the blame and grabs all the credit.

The most important leadership skill for positional leaders is *delegation.* When Bishop Martin Amos of Davenport asked me to develop a leadership training program for his priests, he asked me to emphasize delegation. When we try to do everything by ourselves, we not only wear ourselves out but we also take away opportunities for others to serve and to lead.

People who aspire to servant leadership can evolve, develop, and emerge as servant leaders in one of two ways:

1. Those with positional authority can *step back* from the limelight, *step outside* the box, or *step off* the pedestal and practice servanthood and leadership.

2. Servants who want to bring about change can *step up* and practice leadership.

Leader as Servant

Father Marv Mottet is a servant leader who has positional authority. He is motivated *first to serve and then to lead*. He serves people with charity and leads them toward justice.

Father Mottet is nationally known for his "Two Feet of Christian Service" model and its balanced approach on charity and justice. His model transformed social ministry for religious organizations all over the country. The idea is to walk with the two feet of *charity and justice*—providing directly for people's needs while also addressing the root causes of those needs.

Father Mottet is an excellent mentor who models what he preaches. All the time that he was a pastor, Father Mottet lived and worked among the poor, building hope and providing aid. He didn't stop there. He advocated for changes in political and economic systems to bring about social justice. He started neighbor-

Blessed are Leaders who are Pure of Heart

hood organizations and founded social service agencies to deal with poverty, homelessness, and issues of concern to low-income people.

The cornerstone of his model is to *observe*, *judge*, and *act*. *Observation* is based on the perspective of personal relationships with people who are suffering. *Judgment* is based on careful analysis and prayerful discernment of the gospel. *Action* is based on passionate commitment to a mission, collaborative efforts to involve those who are suffering, and courageous initiatives to create a shared vision to bring about lasting change.

When Father Mottet was named national director of the Catholic Campaign for Human Development, a $13 million-per-year ministry to support ecumenical and interfaith efforts to address the causes of poverty, he chose to live for seven years in one of the poorest neighborhoods in Washington, DC. He could have afforded palatial quarters and justified it by the intense work and travel demands of his job. But instead, he slept on a mattress on the floor of a Catholic Worker House that was providing hospitality and shelter for the homeless.

Most of his work has been done behind the scenes without fanfare or media attention. It was done with the help of thousands of volunteers and hundreds of local leaders, many of whom are personally invited, encouraged, and supported by Father Mottet.

Developing leaders has been the hallmark of this effort. Father Mottet knows how to (1) recruit people with a personal one-on-one request, (2) delegate significant responsibility to them, and (3) provide them with the resources they need to succeed. It is hard to say no to Father Mottet because you know that he is working harder than anyone else.

The need to develop community leaders is why I originally became interested in leadership. With Father Mottet as my mentor and pastor, I realized that an idealistic mission like social change to improve the plight of the poor is a mission in search of many leaders.

The world desperately needs new leaders and new models of leadership. Without leaders, there is no change. The key to bringing about change, whether it is structural, political, strategic, or cultural, is developing leaders to transform these systems. Author James MacGregor Burns asserts that all leadership should ultimately be directed at the transformation of society.

The best test of servant leadership, as author Robert Greenleaf notes, is whether the followers are becoming healthier, wiser, and more likely to become servants and leaders themselves. As I point out in my earlier book, *Servant Leadership Models for Your Parish*, "It is not about how many followers you lead but how many leaders you develop."

Servant as Leader

Two servant leaders developed by Father Mottet are volunteers Glenn Leach and Loxi Hopkins. Glenn retired early from military service to devote his life to charitable work and social justice. Motivated *first to serve and then to lead*, Glenn has devoted more than fifteen years as a full-time volunteer for immigration rights, housing, and disaster relief, among many causes. Glenn practices the spiritual and corporal works of mercy.

For more on servant leadership, visit:

WWW

www.blessingsforleaders.com

Loxi Hopkins is both servant and leader. As a volunteer for Birthright, she provides counseling and assistance to women who are pregnant. As a volunteer for Quad Cities Interfaith, she takes on servant roles such as phoning, taking minutes, and writing letters. She also leads advocacy initiatives, raises funds, and recruits other potential leaders.

Conclusion

Servant leaders can evolve in one of two ways: (1) They can be people in positions of authority who reflect on their leadership style, examine their heart for true motivation, and focus their energy toward service. (2) They can be people without authority whose passion for serving a cause and interest in bringing about change inspire them to lead.

Servant leadership can emerge from anyone, anywhere. Father Mottet illustrates how those with positional authority can have the *wisdom* and *grace* to become leaders who serve. Glenn Leach and Loxi Hopkins demonstrate that those who are already servants can become servants who lead. Interestingly, the more likely the leader is willing to *step back*, *step down*, or *step away*, at least for a while, and interact directly with the people, the more likely the people are to *step up*, take initiative, and become leaders themselves.

Servant leadership begins in that quiet stirring of a pure heart. The single-hearted find wisdom in the stillness of their hearts:

Be still, and know that I am God! (Ps 46:10)
Be still and know that I am.
Be still and know.
Be still.
Be.

Discussion Questions (*"Blessed are the pure in heart"*)

1. How can you monitor the purity of your motives? How can you be sure that you are motivated primarily by a desire to serve others?

2. Do you have people around you who can help you examine your behaviors and reflect on your motives? Do you have a daily routine for self-monitoring?

3. As a leader, what can you do to encourage others to step up and lead? How can you develop others into leaders?

—— *Chapter 7* ——

Peace

Blessed are the peacemakers, for they will be called children of God.
—Matthew 5:9

This Beatitude blesses those who make peace: Peace with God. Peace with themselves. Peace within communities, families, and organizations. Peace with enemies.

Peace emerges from living and leading through all the Beatitudes. Peace is the outcome of living the virtuous life and leading with a sense of mission (poverty of spirit), compassion (those who mourn), humility (meekness), righteousness, mercy, and purity of heart.

Inner peace is a gift from God. As "children of God," the peacemaker finds *rest* in the presence of God. That rest is the fulfillment that comes from a close relationship with God and others. We are at peace with God, with ourselves, and with others.

Outer peace is the resolution of conflicts. The peacemaker is *restless* about conflict. Dom Helder Camara, a Brazilian bishop, says that peacemakers need a *patient impatience*, which is being *impatient* with injustice but *patient* with the process needed to change things.

Peace cannot be dictated by a person in control. Nor can it be experienced as the absence of conflict. Peace is not war. Nor is it harmony. Peace lives in the creative tension that lies between open warfare at one extreme and conflict avoidance on the other.

How Did Jesus Teach This?

"Seek peace, and pursue it" (Ps 34:14).

Jesus lived and led in this creative tension! This is what he meant when he said, "I have not come to bring peace, but a sword" (Matt 10:34). Actually, Jesus brought a "two-edged sword" (Heb 4:12). Peace cuts both ways: neither violence nor avoidance will make peace. Jesus did not come to avoid conflict nor to perpetuate an empty sense of harmony. He generated restlessness with unresolved conflict while insisting on a peaceful means to solve it.

Shalom—the common Jewish greeting—wishes the inner peace of God to those we meet. It also signifies an outer peace that is just and lasting. Jesus longed for a true sense of shalom for Israel. And he wished it upon his disciples with his greeting of shalom (Matt 28:9).

Jesus prepared his disciples to enter a world of conflict. To follow Jesus, we are to be *wise* as serpents and *gentle* as doves (Matt 10:16). We must be willing to take up our cross to follow him (Matt 10:38). Yet we are not to be afraid (Matt 10:26-31). The peace of God will always be with us (Matt 28:20).

Jesus teaches us to make peace with our family, friends, and colleagues: "First be reconciled to your brother or sister, and then come and offer your gift" (Matt 5:24). Peace in the world begins with peace in our families and communities. We learn to love our enemies by loving those around us who are most difficult to love (Matt 5:44).

What Is the Leadership Message?

Conflict happens in all relationships. Conflict happens every day in all organizations. Most of us prefer to steer clear of, get around, or keep away from conflict. When I was in seventh grade, I missed a question on a religion exam that asked, "In the best Christian communities, will there be conflict?" I answered, "No." Funny how I remember that. It is a lesson I have spent a lifetime relearning. When we choose to ignore or avoid conflict, we are not building a healthy community and we are not peacemakers.

Unresolved conflict surrounds us in our nations, communities, neighborhoods, and families. It is the most reducible expense in most organizations. Avoiding conflict is both inefficient and ineffective. Unresolved conflict costs time, energy, and attention.

Conflict can be seen as a problem and an opportunity. When we face conflict squarely, we actually save time and improve relationships. Trust grows. People work together. Teams become more cohesive. Collaboration on future projects becomes more likely.

Emotion and Intentions

Conflict occurs, according to author Kenneth Thomas, when we become aware that someone has done or is going to do something that threatens something we care about. Our thoughts and emotions come immediately into play. Anger, fear, and sadness become a filter for our thoughts. We do not think as clearly. When feelings become intense, they impact and interfere with our thoughts, ideas, and *intentions*.

Purity of heart means we try to purify those intentions. When in conflict, our best intentions can be filtered by our thoughts and emotions. We lose objectivity. Thomas suggests that our *intentions*—and our *responses* to conflict—fall into these five categories:

Accommodation: We just give the other person what he or she wants.

Avoidance: We stay away from the conflict issue altogether.

Compromise: We meet the other person halfway.

Competition: We attack the other person to get what we want.

Collaboration: We figure out a way for both of us to get what we want.

To *collaborate* is more common as an *intention* than as an actual *response* to conflict. When our thoughts and emotions are being flooded by the sudden realization of a conflict, our instinctive reaction is usually either *fight* (to compete) or *flight* (to accommodate or avoid). We either strike back or we retreat into our anger, which turns to frustration, bitterness, and resentment. We feel neglected, betrayed, and afraid. Our fears prevent us from acting assertively (on our own interests) and cooperatively (on the interests of others).

What conflict *avoidance, accommodation*, and *competition* have in common is that none of them requires much in the way of people skills! They are the easy ways out. They do not make for peace. When conflict occurs, it is best to take a *moment of grace* to reflect on our intentions before we respond. Actions and intentions can easily be misunderstood. When strong emotions are in play, our attempts to be kind and merciful can be misconstrued as an attack.

For more on conflict resolution, visit:

www.blessingsforleaders.com

The Neutral Statement of the Conflict

My colleague Randy Richards teaches that it helps to create a neutral statement of the conflict. This is a fair summary of the conflict that both parties can agree to as a starting point for handling their conflict. It clarifies the disagreement, marks the dominant source of conflict, and describes the key differentiator between the two people. These are examples of neutral statements:

"The issue between us is that you want to *satisfy the customer* and I think we should be more concerned about the *profit margin*" (goal conflict).

"The issue is that I think Amy had *better qualifications* than Joe" (factual conflict).

"The issue is that you think what I did was *not fair*" (normative conflict).

Randy suggests that this clarification of the conflict is especially useful because (1) it focuses on the problem without blaming, thus lowering the emotional barriers to working together; and (2) it signals how to move ahead to effectively address the conflict.

Situations can dictate our response to conflict. When we feel strongly about the task, we are more likely to compete. When the relationship is of ultimate importance, we tend to accommodate. When time is tight, we may be forced to compromise (split the difference). When emotions are high, avoidance can make sense as a temporary (but not a final) strategy.

Collaboration

Collaboration is preferable in most situations, especially when dealing with colleagues in an organization. Collaboration is a win-win solution. Randy describes collaboration as *resolution by multiplication*. Both parties win. The organization wins. Compromise, on the other hand, is *resolution by subtraction*. Both parties surrender something.

To become more collaborative, competitors become more cooperative and accommodators become more assertive. Authors Roger Fisher and William Ury call this *principled negotiation*, which is based on the merits of the situation and produces wise, amicable agreements that avoid the costs of giving up or digging in. They suggest the following:

> *Collaboration not only resolves the conflict but it also builds the relationship.*

- Be *hard* on the task without being too hard on the people. The peacemaker attacks the problem without attacking the other person.

- Look for *mutual* gains. The peacemaker knows that in most cases, both sides can win if they work together toward a joint solution.

- Separate the *people* from the *problem*. The peacemaker knows that making the other person the problem just escalates the conflict and erodes the trust. Signs that we are *not* separating the person from the problem include the following:

    We think about the other person as being the problem.

    We say "always" and "never" to describe the other person's behavior.

    We blame the other person for every little thing.

- Focus on *interests*, not positions. The peacemaker is assertive about her or his own interests but not committed to a singular position or solution.

For example, if we both want 100 percent of a truckload of oranges (that is our *position*), we might split the oranges 50-50 (which is a

Interests Matter

compromise). But if your department needs the *insides* of the oranges to make juice, and my department needs the *outsides* of the oranges to make marmalade (that is our *interest*), we can both get 100 percent of what we need (which is *collaboration*).

Surprisingly, differences can lead to creative solutions. If we want *different* parts of the orange, collaboration is more possible. Differences can be based on needs, wants, goals, interests, time, strengths, weaknesses, or resources. To collaborate, we need to think unselfishly about possible solutions, dovetail different interests, invent an abundance of options, and think that solving their problem is also our problem.

Task Conflict and Relationship Conflict

Task conflict occurs when two people have different ideas about how to get the job done. Interestingly, the research by author Karen Jehn shows that moderate to high amounts of task conflict have positive benefits for teams and for organizations, as long as leaders can disentangle the *relationship* aspects of the conflict and focus on the healthy differences about the task.

Relationship conflict occurs when differences go unresolved and we make the other person the problem. Research by Jehn shows that relationship conflict drags down team performance. Relationship conflict neutralizes the positive elements of task conflict because it makes people irritable, frustrated, and resistant to working together. It leads to conflict *escalation*, which occurs when we attack the person instead of attacking the problem at hand.

To maximize opportunities to collaborate, both parties need to be *assertive* about what we want or need (our interests) and *cooperative* about helping the other party get what they want or need (their interests). When in conflict, if I cannot express my own interests, I am not giving you the opportunity to understand and to collaborate on my interests. We need to be aware of, concerned about, and collaborative on the nuances of our own interests *and* those of others.

Hildegard Goss-Mayr

Hildegard Goss-Mayr is collaborative and creative in her approach to conflict. She is one of the most important peacemakers in human history. My friend Richard Deats, in *Marked for Life: The Story of Hildegard Goss-Mayr*, chronicles how Hildegard dedicated her life to peacemaking through the power of nonviolence. For over fifty years, she traveled the globe with her husband, Jean Goss, conducting trainings in nonviolence, teaching conflict resolution, and organizing nonviolent responses to war and injustice. In May 2009, I interviewed Hildegard at her home in Vienna, Austria. While much has been written about Hildegard, I asked her about her teaching methods, especially as they relate to leadership.

Hildegard is a soft-spoken yet charismatic teacher of peace. The first step toward making peace is "to *change yourself*," says Hildegard. Before you can change your social or political reality, you need internal change. She draws from Hebrew Scripture, the Buddha, Lao Tsu, Confucius, and mostly the Sermon on the Mount of Jesus to guide this personal, inward journey for the participants in her trainings.

The second step is *personal reflection on a local conflict or injustice*. Hildegard is invited into areas of heavy conflict, severe poverty, or grave injustice. Her role is to help develop a grassroots response. She asks her participants to get very specific about their situation.

The third step in her change process is *dialogue about the conflict*. Dialogue requires reflection and understanding of the viewpoint of your opponent. This creates an analysis that goes beyond the singular perspective that characterizes most discussions.

The fourth step, and most powerful, is to *role-play the local situation*. Her husband Jean would insist that the group role-play not just once but "over and over until they got it right." The power of the role-play is to understand more fully what the other party to the conflict is thinking, feeling, and most likely doing in the conflict.

The final step is further *dialogue* about the process and what was learned. The group then moves on to another source of conflict, another injustice, or another local problem and goes through the same steps. The iterative process of these trainings takes days, weeks, or even months. This is how she and Jean were successful in organizing nonviolent responses to conflict in many areas around the world, particularly the Philippines, South Africa, Korea, Eastern Europe, and all across Latin America and East Africa.

Hildegard believes that change occurs from both the top-down and the bottom-up. In addition to the grassroots trainings she conducted, Hildegard met with, worked with, and changed the attitudes of presidents and bishops, governors and generals. She told me that she was once told by the president of Argentina, "You cannot govern with the Sermon on the Mount," to which she replied, "You cannot be a Christian without it." It is through the integration of faith and works that Hildegard finds the wisdom of God in her peacemaking.

One of her greatest contributions was the change she inspired in some bishops, including Archbishop Oscar Romero of El Salvador and Cardinal Jaime Sin of the Philippines. Her work helped deepen their view of the gospel as it applies to the social reality of the people.

Dom Helder Camara, the bishop of Recife, Brazil, once left one of her training sessions smiling and proclaiming, "Now I am a nonviolent bishop," to which Jean replied, "Not until you do something." Dom Helder fed the hungry and built houses for the poor but became even more famous for changing social structures that keep people in poverty. He once stated, "I fed the poor and they called me a saint. I asked why they were poor and they called me a Communist."

Dialogue works. Hildegard showed this. Hard bargaining does not work. When we compete, it creates winners and losers. It provokes hostility and becomes a contest of wills. Each party takes an extreme position and holds out longer to get its own way.

Soft bargaining does not work either. When we avoid or accommodate too quickly, we may create temporary harmony but not peace. If we make too many concessions to get an amicable agreement, we might resent the decision because our needs are not being met.

Generally speaking, neither hard nor soft bargaining resolves the task side of the conflict. Nor do they build the working relationship. As author Kerry Patterson and others point out, the *flight to silence* masks the problem and withdraws us from the situation. The *flight to violence* forces our solution, builds resentment, and reduces the opportunity for creative work.

Conclusion

Conflict happens. Peacemakers do not ignore, avoid, or deny the presence of conflict. They *normalize* conflict. Engage it. Act on it. Work through it. They are *assertive but not selfish* about their interests. They are *cooperative but not selfless* in weighing the interests of others. Peacemakers find that wise balance of being both assertive and cooperative at the same time.

Peace unites us toward the common goal necessary for leadership. Peace is not the absence of conflict but the *presence of justice.* Peacemaking is a continuous process. The blessing of this Beatitude is the closer relationship we can build with God and others. That is the gift that comes from consistent efforts to collaborate on the conflicts that fill our world.

Discussion Questions (*"Blessed are the peacemakers"*)

1. How do you respond to conflict? When you are not collaborating, are you more likely to avoid, accommodate, or compete when you are in conflict?

2. What situational factors might change your approach to conflict? In what situations might you tend to be more avoidant? more agreeable? more competitive?

3. Why do you think Jesus calls peacemakers the *children of God*?

—— *Chapter 8* ——

Courage

Blessed are those who are persecuted for righteousness' sake, for theirs is the kingdom of heaven.
—*Matthew 5:10*

If we live and lead by the first seven Beatitudes, we should expect to experience resistance, criticism, and even persecution. Notice that the blessing associated with this Beatitude is the same as the first Beatitude: "Theirs is the kingdom of heaven" (Matt 5:3 and 5:10).

Paradoxically, persecution in this world is a mark of the kingdom of God. Disciples of Jesus should expect to be insulted and ridiculed (Matt 5:11). Such treatment may be a sign that we are on the right track. It can be a test of our faithfulness, a means to our holiness.

To endure persecution for the sake of a higher cause is to grow in faith, hope, and love. Saint Paul drives home this message in his letter to the Romans: "Therefore, since we are justified by faith, we have peace . . . knowing that suffering produces endurance, and endurance produces character, and character produces hope, and hope does not disappoint us, because God's love has been poured into our hearts" (Rom 5:1-5). The trials of our faith become opportunities to grow in *faith, hope,* and *love.*

Those who are *righteous* will be opposed by those who prefer their own self-centered and self-righteous ways of doing things. The positional leaders of Jerusalem in the time of Jesus led with hypocrisy and self-righteousness (Matt 23). Jesus called them "blind guides of the blind" (Matt 15:14). Jesus said they "neglected the weightier matters of the law: justice and mercy and faith" (Matt 23:23).

How Did Jesus Teach This?

Jesus gave hope and courage to his disciples by painting a clear sense of *vision*. Each of the eight Beatitudes concludes with a short *vision statement* from Jesus:

- The poor in spirit will gain the kingdom of heaven.

- Those who mourn will be comforted.

- The meek will inherit the earth.

- Those who hunger for righteousness will be satisfied.

- Those who show mercy will be shown mercy.

- The pure of heart will see God.

- The peacemakers will be called children of God.

- Those persecuted for the sake of righteousness will gain the kingdom of heaven.

Paradoxically, the blessing of each Beatitude is discovered in the process of living and leading by that Beatitude. The means are consistent with the end results. The path leads to the vision. Like an acorn that becomes an oak tree, the seed of truth bears the fruit of the kingdom.

The *vision statements* that conclude each Beatitude are consistent with Jesus' *parables of the kingdom*. In these parables, the kingdom of God is likened to

- a mustard seed, small in size but grows into the largest of shrubs (Matt 13:31-32);

- yeast, a hidden substance that raises the dough when making bread (Matt 13:33);

- a hidden treasure, hard to find yet rich beyond imagination (Matt 13:44);

- fine pearls, when found, that a merchant sells everything to buy (Matt 13:45-46).

Like the Beatitudes, the kingdom *parables* reflect the *paradox* of the kingdom of God. As a leader, Jesus shares his vision in the Beatitudes and in these parables.

What Is the Leadership Message?

The essence of all leadership is influence, change, and vision. Leaders *influence* people by affecting a *change* of heart, mind, spirit, and action. They *transform* organizations and communities by changing policies, structures, strategies, and culture. They *facilitate* a process where the group co-creates the vision, one that is based on the mission.

To lead people through a change process, leaders need courage to overcome resistance to change. A clear sense of vision can break down the resistance to change. Seeing is believing. Organizational change is less stressful for most people when the vision is clear.

Blessed are Leaders who are Persecuted for the Sake of Righteousness

Vision articulates what success would look like if the mission is accomplished. It is the end result, a picture of ultimate success. Vision generates clarity, focus, and power to provide more service for the benefit of all. That power is freely given and shared, not hoarded. Power grows out of a shared vision. People are thus empowered to perform their roles.

Vision provides a sense of direction. While mission creates a sense of *purpose*, vision is about future *direction*: Where are we going? What are our goals? Like a driver who can go faster when the windshield of a car is clear of ice and snow, the people in an organization can go faster and be more productive when they have a clear vision of where they are moving.

Mission and Vision

Mission and vision articulate the task side of leadership. If leaders are only concerned about relationships and not the task, we might as well be organizing a social club or talking football around the watercooler all day. Remember: the leader needs to be equally concerned about the task (the job that needs to be done) *and* the relationship (the people and how they relate to each other) in order to be an effective leader.

Results Matter

A quick glance at internet sites demonstrates that most organizations confuse mission and vision. Through my experiences with facilitating strategic planning since the 1980s, I have learned that few people really understand the difference between mission and vision.

The mission is like an anchor that keeps the organization grounded. The *mission statement* has three parts: business, purpose, and values. It is written in the present tense.

The vision is like the north star that keeps the organization heading in the right direction. The *vision statement* is written in the future tense. It does not need to describe or explain the entire vision (that is the strategic plan). It simply captures its core essence. It paints a picture of the new direction the organization wants to go.

Both mission and vision are consistent with the core values. Both address the common good by describing how society as a whole benefits from this organization.

An *internal vision statement* describes what the organization will look like if it accomplishes its mission. An *external vision statement* describes how the *world* will look if the organization accomplishes its mission. This is a huge difference!

The internal vision statement is more common. It answers the question, How will our organization be better off if we accomplish our mission? It usually goes something like, "This organization will be recognized as a leader in its field" or "We will be #1 in our class" or "We will beat our competitor." A quick glance at vision statements shows an excessive use of words like best, first, foremost, leading, and premier.

For more on vision statements, visit:

WW W
www.blessingsforleaders.com

Let's say that a company has a vision statement that says, "Beat X" (its competitor). This might excite some workers at the company, but it does nothing to inspire anyone else to buy its products. Why should we care if that company beats another? Now, if the vision statement speaks to our human condition in some way, addressing how the products could improve our health or meet our needs, we might be inspired by its vision.

The external vision statement is more powerful. It answers the question, How will *the world* be better off if we accomplish our mission? It speaks to the common good. It addresses how mission success will benefit others, not just the company. This can truly be motivating for the people both inside *and* outside the organization.

Crawford Company

The Crawford Company of Rock Island, Illinois, is an excellent example of *participative* strategic planning and visioning. Their core business is heating, air-conditioning, air-cleaning systems, and plumbing. They did an excellent job of involving virtually every employee in every step of their planning.

Crawford Mission Statement: We solve problems by customizing quality services and dependable products to fit the needs of our customers.

First, nearly all eighty workers participated in core values work-shops. These sessions helped articulate Crawford's *mission statement* and *values statement*. In the process, they also built greater understanding, appreciation, and commitment to the mission and values. Several employees volunteered to help draft the statements.

Crawford Core Values Statement:

Teamwork: We work together as one team aimed at reaching common goals.

Innovation: We are flexible and resourceful in discovering innovative solutions.

Quality: We strive to deliver the highest quality products and dependable services.

Customer Service: We act with the utmost professionalism in serving our customers.

Integrity: We show what we believe by practicing these values.

Crawford employees were also involved in focus groups to collect the data by doing some assessment, analysis, and visioning. Every employee was invited to attend, and almost every employee attended one of the sessions. This gave us background information for the environmental assessment, where the strengths, weaknesses, opportunities, and threats (SWOT) are identified before the *strategic issues* are deciphered (below).

Based on the SWOT, we discovered four strategic issues that needed attention. These were framed as questions in order to set up the next step in the process: developing *strategies*.

Crawford Strategic Issues:

1. How can we continue to grow as an entrepreneurial company?

2. How can we make more efficient use of our physical space and possibly expand to accommodate our growth?

3. How can we continuously improve our use of technology?

4. How can we strengthen our human resource (H.R.) function?

For each of these questions, we brainstormed several possible ways of answering the question. These become *strategies*, and we prioritized about three strategies per strategic issue. The final step of the

For more on strategic planning, visit:

www.blessingsforleaders.com

strategic planning process is identifying several *action steps* for each strategy. These are very specific: Basically, who is going to do what by when?

The Ebener-Smith Model of Strategic Planning

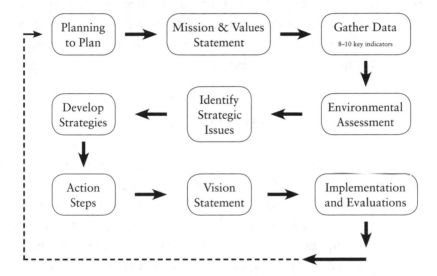

At Crawford, when we worked on the strategic issues, strategies, and action steps, the owners called different employees into the meeting to receive their input at various steps along the way. In fact, some of the employees helped write certain parts of the strategic plan.

By involving so many people, Crawford created a sense of *shared vision* for the company. As author Peter Drucker stated, "You cannot predict the future but you can create it" (Cohen, *Drucker on Leadership*). This famous dictum suggests that people working, planning, and visioning together can create a sense of vision together, as they did at Crawford. By building it together, the workers have more ownership in the strategic plan and the vision. Note that the vision comes at the end of the strategic planning process, not the beginning, so it is built step-by-step by the whole group.

> Crawford Vision Statement: Our customers, our employees and our company will prosper as we deliver quality services and dependable products.

When writing the vision statement, the owners at Crawford practiced *participatory leadership* one more time. They did speak of profitability, as that is an important bottom line for all for-profits. But they also spoke of sharing that profit with employees, customers, and the community. This is *going beyond the bottom line*. It speaks to support for the common good.

Shared Vision

Vision is the common goal required of leadership: *leading is the interactive process of influencing a group of people in the direction of a common goal*. Without a common goal, or a shared vision, the process might be management. It might be coercion. It might be commandership. But it is *not* leadership: without the *shared* aspect of the vision or *common* aspect of the goal, it is not leadership.

Goals can be a powerful motivator when the people buy into the goals. The path-goal theory suggests that people with strong internal drive (which is wanted) are motivated when they are personally involved in setting and pursuing challenging goals.

People with an *internal* locus of control believe that their actions make a real difference. They believe that they are making more of an impact on people and events around them. (People with an *external* locus of control see it the other way around.) People with an internal locus of control want to be involved in setting goals and making decisions that affect their work.

Leaders can internalize locus of control by involving their people in setting goals, making decisions, and solving problems. They evaluate progress toward these goals and recognize people for their accomplishments. They show people how they make a difference.

Strategic Thinking and Doing

Leaders continue to think and act strategically after the formal process of strategic planning. David O'Connell, the dean of my College of Business, is tenacious about keeping the strategic issues, strategies, and action steps in front of his faculty whenever we meet. He finds multiple ways of keeping the mission, vision, and values statements in front of all of us. He mounts them on the wall, adds them to his stationery, and refers to them in his presentations.

Without leadership, strategic plans will fail. Leaders like Cheryl Goodwin of Family Resources understand that strategy is a process of *continuous improvement.* She involves her board, staff, and leadership team in many aspects of strategic planning, such as

- using the strategic plan as the focal point for board and staff meetings;

- evaluating and updating the strategic plan;

- monitoring the outside environment;

- naming and acting upon the *adaptive* challenges.

Adaptive planning focuses on those challenges for which there is no quick fix or technical solution. According to author Ronald Heifetz, examples include changes in attitude, behavior, or culture that become necessary because of *external* changes, things going on in the outside environment that threaten the very livelihood of our organization. As author John Kotter emphasizes, leaders fight complacency by creating a *sense of urgency* about the need for change.

Leaders bring about change.

Entropy is a biological concept that suggests that every living organism is in the process of dying. If we think of our organizations as living organisms, then they too can become the victims of entropy. Leaders breathe new life into organizations by insisting that the people and the organization need to *adapt* to changes in the outside environment. Given the speed and complexity of external change today, leaders need to stimulate internal change to keep up. The basic idea is that if your organization is not changing and growing, it is dying.

Conclusion

Maintaining a sense of urgency about organizational change is a daunting task. Change agents will face complacency, apathy, and resistance. That is why leaders need *courage*, *commitment*, and *clarity of vision* to lessen the fear of the people. They need the *fortitude* to keep the heat on but the *wisdom* to prevent the temperature from getting too hot.

Leaders are missionaries and visionaries. To maintain zeal for the mission and focus on the vision requires tenacity, stamina, and courage. Leaders who practice the counter-intuitive and counter-cultural ways of Jesus will encounter the harsh realities of criticism, resistance, and even persecution. But Jesus tells us, "Take heart, it is I; do not be afraid" (Matt 14:27).

Discussion Questions
(*"Blessed are those who are persecuted for righteousness' sake"*)

1. What sort of adversity do you face for standing up for what you believe in?

2. As a leader, how do you create a sense of shared vision? How well do you involve others in goal setting?

3. It takes both insight and foresight to do strategic planning. How can you improve your leadership skills of insight and foresight?

The Apostolic Challenge of Leadership

Teach me, O Lord, the wisdom of your ways.
—based on Psalm 25:4

T he word *disciple* means one who is *called forth to learn and follow*. In the Great Invitation, Jesus calls us to *come forth and follow* him (Matt 4:18-20). The word *apostle* means one who is *sent forth*. In the Great Commission, Jesus calls us to *go forth and teach* all nations all that he taught (Matt 28:18-20), especially the Great Commandment to love (Matt 22:32-40).

Jesus prepared his disciples for the challenges of life and leadership. He gave us the Beatitudes to share the wisdom of the psalms, proverbs, and prophets. Here we found insight from the virtues of the Beatitudes and applied that to leadership.

In the story of the Great Commission (Matt 28:16-20), Jesus shows that the role of a disciple is to *become an apostle*. The role of an apostle is to *develop more disciples*. In the same way that leaders transform followers into leaders, Jesus transformed disciples into apostles.

Transforming Followers into Leaders

My students come from all walks of life. The diversity of students in a leadership classroom is one of the reasons I love to teach

83

organizational leadership. All sorts of organizations are looking for leaders and trying to improve on their leadership. Most of my students rise to positions of authority because they have good technical skills as engineers, soldiers, ministers, doctors, nurses, teachers, accountants, cooks, social workers, and so forth.

Subject-matter experts become managers in most professions. Managers are asked to become leaders. One of my students is an expert in truck parts and was promoted to manager of maintenance. She went from managing trucks to leading people. Another student excelled as a waitress. They made her a manager and then expected her to lead.

Leadership is like parenting in two ways. First, neither comes with an instruction manual. Rarely do my students receive enough preparation, training, or support when they are promoted. Second, leadership should be a *process of gradually letting go*. Like parents, who gradually let go of their children, leaders should let go of their followers and develop them into leaders. The *cycle of leadership development* that I propose is this:

1. New leaders receive plenty of mentoring and coaching to guide, teach, evaluate, and encourage them for about two years, with increasing responsibility and complexity.

2. In time and with experience, leaders practice with less coaching.

3. At some point, proficient leaders become mentors and coaches to guide, teach, evaluate, and encourage others—while continuing to receive some coaching as well.

The *challenge of leadership* is to transform followers into leaders. The *challenge of apostleship* is to transform disciples into apostles, ones who are ready, willing, and able to lead. We need mentors and role models, coaches and trainers, teachers and supervisors who

- recognize the gifts and talents of their followers;

- delegate meaningful work while providing support and feedback;

- guide, teach, encourage, and evaluate progress;

- lift up followers to become leaders.

Beatitudes Leadership

The Beatitudes are eight blessings for leaders. As we reflect on them each and every day, the Beatitudes challenge us to deepen our faith, strengthen our relationships, and strive to improve on our leadership practices. No matter what we did yesterday, no matter how well or how poorly we performed today, we will get a new set of opportunities to lead tomorrow.

The Chinese word for *crisis* also means *opportunity*. Embedded in every crisis is an opportunity to change. Tomorrow will bring new conflicts, new challenges, and new crises that can be seen as opportunities. Every morning, we start anew. With the Beatitudes as our guide, we can monitor, reflect, and improve on that next opportunity to lead.

Every leadership challenge or management situation offers a basic choice:

- Is this an opportunity to practice my faith? Or do I separate my faith life from the other parts of my life?

- Do I abide by the business culture of our secular society? Or do I consider the counter-cultural ways of the Beatitudes?

- Do I follow my own selfish instincts? Or do I practice the counter-intuitive ways of the Beatitudes?

A growing body of research shows that putting people ahead of profits can be profitable. Putting mission ahead of money can raise money. But only if that effort is genuine.

The paradox here is that practicing the virtuous leadership of the Beatitudes can also be the most effective approach. We can practice our faith as we face the challenges of organizational life and, at the same time, enhance the effectiveness of our organizations.

Efficiency and effectiveness are guiding principles for managers and leaders. Author Peter Drucker stated that *managers value efficiency* and *leaders value effectiveness*. Managers *do things right* and do them efficiently, while leaders *do the right things* and do them effectively. Leadership effectiveness *and* managerial efficiency are both critical to the success of our organizations. Both are *necessary* and neither is *sufficient*.

The choice is not between being faithful to the gospel *or* being effective and efficient. The Beatitudes leader can be faithful *and* effective. The Beatitudes manager can be faithful *and* efficient. These are not either/or questions. To think you have to choose between being faithful *or* doing what is in the best interests of your organization is another false dichotomy.

We have made a science of command and control tactics. It is easier to command and control than to lead. Leadership is more difficult than coercion. The most important jobs of leadership cannot be coerced. We cannot command people to trust us. We cannot control whether people are kind and merciful to each other.

Leaders inspire, invite, and persuade. They do not coerce. Most of us prefer to be inspired, invited, or persuaded than coerced. Noncoercive people skills produce better decisions, performance, and relationships. Working with people is sometimes called the *soft skills*, but as my friend Randy Richards likes to say, they should be called the *complex people skills*.

In most management workshops or training sessions, the learning outcomes are related to technical or managerial skills that enhance efficiency or explain procedures. This book looked at the wisdom of Jesus for insight into how we nurture the values, practice the virtues, and develop the inner character to *change the way we live, lead, manage, and follow*. We explored how Jesus would lead and what Jesus would do in management and leadership settings.

The *paradoxes of leadership* can be understood from a careful reflection on the Beatitudes. Leading by the Beatitudes is not the easy path, but it can be the most fulfilling. It takes *wisdom, empathy, humility, justice, mercy, service, peace*, and *courage*:

1. The leader is *poor in spirit*: nurtures a closer relationship with God through prayer and reflection, and recognizes divine providence when it is at work.

2. The leader is *able to mourn*: able to empathize with the people and relate to where they are coming from, where they are, and where they are going.

3. The leader is *meek*: humble enough to involve the people in the process of making decisions, solving problems, and addressing challenges.

4. The leader seeks *right relationships*: builds integrity, credibility, and a good reputation, which is based on character, hard work, and virtuous living.

5. The leader is *merciful*: willing and able to work through the mistakes that happen when followers are empowered to take risks and show creative initiative.

6. The leader strives for *purity of heart*: motivated first to serve, totally devoted to a mission, the leader steps down to serve and the follower steps up to lead.

7. The leader is a *peacemaker*: promotes peaceful resolution of conflict, never settling for empty harmony or allowing unresolved conflicts to fester.

8. The leader is willing to risk *persecution*: overcomes resistance to change by courageously pursuing a vision that is created and shared by the whole team.

As Jesus concludes the Beatitudes, "Blessed are you when people revile you and persecute you and utter all kinds of evil against you falsely on my account. Rejoice and be glad, for your reward is great in heaven, for in the same way they persecuted the prophets who were before you" (Matt 5:11-12).

———

> *Discipleship evolves into apostleship just as sure as followership evolves into leadership.*

We have journeyed through the Gospel of Matthew, especially his Beatitudes, to look for insights into leadership. Interestingly, the Gospel of Matthew is very appropriate for leadership studies because leadership is a recurring theme. Matthew describes an intimate relationship between Jesus and the Twelve, the apostles he was training for leadership.

Beatitudes leaders transform themselves, the people around them, the organizations they lead, and the communities they serve. As author Bernard Bass points out, transformational leaders intrinsically motivate their followers. They *transform followers into leaders.*

The Beatitudes are guiding principles for Christian life as well as leadership. The person who wants to be blessed can do so by *living and leading* with the Beatitudes.

There is a sense of joy that comes from leading without controlling, compelling, or coercing others to follow. We can invite, influence, and inspire others with a shared vision that builds hope for a better future. If we wish to model the way that God enters our lives in loving, truthful, and beautiful ways, we can lead with the wisdom from these Beatitudes.

As Saint Paul writes in his letter to the Colossians,

> As God's chosen ones, holy and beloved, clothe yourselves with compassion, kindness, humility, meekness, and patience. Bear with one another and, if anyone has a complaint against another, forgive each other; just as the Lord has forgiven you, so you also must forgive. Above all, clothe yourselves with love, which binds everything together in perfect harmony. (Col 3:12-14)

For more information, go to the website at:

www.blessingsforleaders.com

Bibliography

Introduction

Aquinas, T. (1920). *The Summa Theologica of St. Thomas Aquinas*. Vols. 1–5. Rev. ed. London: Burns, Oates & Washburne.

Forest, J. (1999). *The Ladder of the Beatitudes*. Maryknoll, NY: Orbis.

Katz, R. L. (1955). "Skills of an Effective Administrator." *Harvard Business Review*, 33 (1), 33–42.

Rost, J. C. (1991). *Leadership for the Twenty-First Century*. New York: Praeger.

Chapter 1

Allison, M., and Kaye, J. (2005). *Strategic Planning for Nonprofit Organizations: A Practical Guide and Workbook*. Hoboken, NJ: Support Center for Non-profit Management, John Wiley.

Rost, J. C. (1991). *Leadership for the Twenty-First Century*. New York: Praeger.

United States Conference of Catholic Bishops (1986). *Economic Justice for All*. Washington, DC: USCCB.

Chapter 2

Goleman, D. (1998). *Working with Emotional Intelligence*. New York: Bantam.

Heifetz, R. A. (1994). *Leadership without Easy Answers*. Cambridge, MA: Harvard University Press.

Pope John Paul II (1988). "On Social Concerns." *Population & Development Review*, 14 (1), 211–17.

Chapter 3

Chaleff, I. (2003). *The Courageous Follower: Standing Up To & For Our Leaders*. San Francisco: Berrett-Koehler.

Collins, J. C. (2001). *Good to Great: Why Some Companies Make the Leap and Others Don't*. New York: HarperCollins.

Crosby, M. H. (1981). *Spirituality of the Beatitudes: Matthew's Vision for the Church in an Unjust World*. Maryknoll, NY: Orbis.

Fisher, R., Ury, W., and Patton, B. (1991). *Getting to YES: Negotiating Agreement Without Giving In*. New York: Penguin.

Forest, J. (1999). *The Ladder of the Beatitudes*. Maryknoll, NY: Orbis.

Heider, F. (1958). *The Psychology of Interpersonal Relations*. Hoboken, NJ: John Wiley.

Kelley, R. E. (1992). *The Power of Followership*. New York: Doubleday.

Lefton, R. E., and Buzzotta, V. R. (2004). *Leadership through People Skills: Using the Dimensional Model of Behavior to Help Managers*. New York: McGraw-Hill.

Lencioni, P. (2002). *The Five Dysfunctions of a Team*. San Francisco: Jossey-Bass.

Chapter 4

Aquinas, T. (1920). *The Summa Theologica of St. Thomas Aquinas*. Vols. 1–5. Rev. ed. London: Burns, Oates & Washburne.

Cohen, W. A. (2010). *Drucker on Leadership: New Lessons from the Father of Modern Management*. San Francisco: Jossey-Bass.

Kotter, J. P. (1997). *Leading Change*. Cambridge, MA: Harvard Business School Press.

Kouzes, J. M., and Posner, B. Z. (2003). *The Leadership Challenge: How to Keep Getting Extraordinary Things Done in Organizations*. San Francisco: Jossey-Bass.

Lefton, R. E., and Buzzotta, V. R. (2004). *Leadership through People Skills: Using the Dimensional Model of Behavior to Help Managers*. New York: McGraw-Hill.

Chapter 5

Bass, B. M. (1985). *Leadership and Performance Beyond Expectations*. New York: Free Press.

Blake, R. R., and Mouton, J. S. (1964). *The Managerial Grid.* Houston: Gulf Publishing.

Ebener, D. R. (2010). *Servant Leadership Models for Your Parish.* Mahwah, NJ: Paulist Press.

Hersey, P., and Blanchard, K. H. (1969). *Management of Organizational Behavior: Utilizing Human Resources.* Englewood Cliffs, NJ: Prentice Hall.

Jehn, K. A. (1995). "A Multimethod Examination of the Benefits and Detriments of Intragroup Conflict." *Administrative Science Quarterly,* 4 (2), 256–82.

Lefton, R. E., and Buzzotta, V. R. (2004). *Leadership through People Skills: Using the Dimensional Model of Behavior to Help Managers.* New York: McGraw-Hill.

Organ, D. W. (1988). *Organizational Citizenship Behavior: The Good Soldier Syndrome.* Lexington, MA: Lexington Books.

Chapter 6

Barach, J. A., and Eckhardt, D. R. (1996). "The Paradoxes of Leadership." In G. R. Hickman, ed., *Leading Organizations: Perspective for a New Era,* 68–78. Thousand Oaks, CA: Sage Publications.

Blanchard, K., and Hodges, P. (2005). *Lead Like Jesus: Lessons from the Greatest Role Model of All Time.* Nashville: Thomas Nelson.

Burns, J. (1978). *Leadership.* New York: Harper & Row.

Collins, J. C. (2001). *Good to Great: Why Some Companies Make the Leap and Others Don't.* New York: HarperCollins.

Deats, R. (2003). *Martin Luther King, Jr.: Spirit-Led Prophet.* New City, NY: New City Press.

Ebener, D. R. (2010). *Servant Leadership Models for Your Parish.* Mahwah, NJ: Paulist Press.

———. (2011). "On Becoming a Servant Leader: Seven Myths and Seven Paradoxes of Christian Leadership." *Sojourners* (February 2011): 33–34.

Greenleaf, R. K. (2003). *The Servant Leader Within: A Transformative Path.* Mahwah, NJ: Paulist Press.

Keith, K. M. (2008). *The Case for Servant Leadership.* Westfield, IN: Greenleaf Center for Servant Leadership.

Muto, S. A. (1982). *Blessings That Make Us Be: A Formative Approach to Living the Beatitudes*. New York: Crossroads.

Phelps, O. (2009). *The Catholic Vision for Leading Like Jesus: Introducing S³ Leadership: Servant, Steward, Shepherd*. Huntington, IN: Our Sunday Visitor.

Rost, J. C. (1991). *Leadership for the Twenty-First Century*. New York: Praeger.

Sashkin, M., and Sashkin, M. G. (2003). *Leadership That Matters: The Critical Factors for Making a Difference in People's Lives and Organizations' Success*. San Francisco: Berrett-Koehler.

Chapter 7

Deats, R. (2009). *Marked for Life: The Story of Hildegard Goss-Mayr*. New City, NY: New City Press.

De Broucker, J. (1970). *Dom Helder Camara: The Violence of a Peacemaker*. Maryknoll, NY: Orbis.

Fisher, R., Ury, W., and Patton, B. (1991). *Getting to YES: Negotiating Agreement Without Giving In*. New York: Penguin.

Glasl, F. (1999). *Confronting Conflict: A First-Aid Kit for Handling Conflict*. Gloucestershire, England: Hawthorn Press.

Jehn, K. A. (1995). "A Multimethod Examination of the Benefits and Detriments of Intragroup Conflict." *Administrative Science Quarterly*, 4 (2): 256–82.

Patterson, K., Grenny, J., McMillan, R., and Switztler, A. (2002). *Crucial Conversations: Tools for Talking When Stakes Are High*. New York: McGraw-Hill.

Thomas, K. W. (1992). "Conflict and Negotiation Processes in Organizations." In M. D. Dunnette, L. M. Hough, *Handbook of Industrial and Organizational Psychology*, 3 (2nd ed.), 651–717.

United States Conference of Catholic Bishops (1983). *The Challenge of Peace: God's Promise and Our Response*. Washington, DC: USCCB.

Chapter 8

Bryson, J. M., and Alston, F. K. (2004). *Creating and Implementing Your Strategic Plan: A Workbook for Public and Nonprofit Organizations*. 2nd ed. San Francisco: Jossey-Bass.

Cohen, W. A. (2010). *Drucker on Leadership: New Lessons from the Father of Modern Management*. San Francisco: Jossey-Bass.

Heifetz, R. A. (1994). *Leadership Without Easy Answers*. Cambridge, MA: Harvard University Press.

Kotter, J. P. (1997). *Leading Change*. Cambridge, MA: Harvard Business School Press.

Conclusion

Bass, B. M., and Avolio, B. J. (1994). *Improving Organizational Effectiveness through Transformational Leadership*. Thousand Oaks, CA: Sage Publications.

Burns, J. (1978). *Leadership*. New York: Harper & Row.

Cohen, W. A. (2010). *Drucker on Leadership: New Lessons from the Father of Modern Management*. San Francisco: Jossey-Bass.

Keith, K. M. (2008). *The Case for Servant Leadership*. Westfield, IN: Greenleaf Center for Servant Leadership.